How to Beat

Agoraphobia

Also in the series

How to Beat Depression and Persistent Low Mood
Mark Papworth

How to Beat Fears and Phobias
Mark Papworth

How to Beat Insomnia and Sleep Problems
Kirstie Anderson

PAMELA MYLES-HOOTON

How to Beat
Agoraphobia

ROBINSON

ROBINSON

First published in Great Britain in 2021 by Robinson
This edition published in 2023 by Robinson

1 3 5 7 9 10 8 6 4 2

Previously published as *How to Beat Agoraphobia One Step at a Time*

Copyright © Pamela Myles-Hooton, 2021

The moral right of the author has been asserted.

Important Note
This book is not intended as a substitute for medical advice or
treatment. Any person with a condition requiring medical attention
should consult a qualified medical practitioner
or suitable therapist.

A CIP catalogue record for this book
is available from the British Library.

ISBN: 978-1-47214-836-0

Typeset in Minion by Initial Typesetting Services, Edinburgh
Printed and bound in Great Britain by Clays Ltd, Elcograf S.p.A.

Papers used by Robinson are from well-managed forests
and other responsible sources.

Robinson
An imprint of
Little, Brown Book Group
Carmelite House
50 Victoria Embankment
London EC4Y 0DZ

An Hachette UK Company
www.hachette.co.uk

www.littlebrown.co.uk

This book is written in loving memory of my dear husband Robert Myles-Hooton.

I dedicate this book to Rob's mum, Ann Hooton.

CONTENTS

GETTING GOING

Well done for making the first step!

Sometimes the hardest step is the first one. I am sorry that you are struggling with agoraphobia, which is likely to be having a severe impact on your daily life, but glad that you have started reading this book. You have taken the first and one of the most important steps towards your journey to recovery. The book is designed to teach you evidence-based techniques to enable you to face your fears. Some people have this type of problem for many years and say that it severely restricts their ability to enjoy life. Often, in order to get better, we first have to reach a point where we are willing to invest time and energy in the task of addressing the problem. This is because psychological approaches usually involve a great deal of personal effort which is needed to reap the full benefit of what they have to offer. So, before we start, do please think about whether you have this time and effort available. I'll talk more about this later in the chapter.

The strategies in this book are based on the principles of cognitive behavioural therapy (CBT), an evidence-based psychological treatment that has been shown to help people with this type of problem. The book is divided into sections that you can work through at a pace that suits you. There are also two case studies of people with agoraphobia who have used the strategies in this book. Although these are fictitious characters, they are based on the stories of real people and their recovery stories show how each of them was able to put the techniques into action to improve their lives.

About me

First of all, I should introduce myself and explain a bit about who I am and why I have written this book. I am an accredited cognitive behavioural therapist, trainer and supervisor and for more than thirty years I have been helping people with problems like yours. I co-wrote *The CBT Handbook*, which has been used by many people to overcome problems with anxiety, depression and anger. I spent over eleven years training others in delivering evidence-based interventions for people with common mental health problems at the University of Reading, and latterly I have worked with NHS Education for Scotland to develop a training programme for mental health staff who help people experiencing anxiety and depression. Outside of work I enjoy cooking, gardening, pastel drawing and spending time with my two dogs.

What is agoraphobia?

Agoraphobia is a fear of being in situations in which the person believes that escape may be difficult or that help will not be available if something goes wrong. Many people think that it is simply a fear of open spaces, but it isn't: it's more complicated than that. Agoraphobia actually translates from Greek as 'fear of the marketplace'. Many people with agoraphobia find it difficult to use public transport, go shopping at the supermarket or shopping centre, or even leave home without being accompanied by someone they trust. If a person with agoraphobia finds themselves in a situation such as this, they may experience physical symptoms of panic, including racing heart (palpitations), rapid breathing (hyperventilating), feeling hot and sweaty, feeling sick, butterflies in the tummy and diarrhoea.

Symptoms of agoraphobia

People with agoraphobia will tend to *avoid* a wide range of situations (e.g. queues, public transport, large crowded shops, supermarkets, shopping centres, theatres, cinemas, etc.). In these situations, the person will commonly feel some or even all of the *physical symptoms* of anxiety and panic listed in the previous paragraph (e.g. palpitations, hyperventilation, etc.). More on these unpleasant symptoms in Section 2. When the person is feeling this way, they will often fear that something bad is going to happen and might have upsetting *thoughts* such as 'I'm going to faint', 'I'm going to have a heart attack', 'I'm going to stop breathing', 'I'm going to fall over', etc.). Having these very unpleasant physical symptoms and frightening thoughts can lead to an increase in the person's *feelings* of anxiety and panic. As a way of coping, many people use what we call *safety behaviours*, which tend to help the person to feel less anxious and might include things like always being accompanied when out, carrying medication, a bottle of water or even a good luck charm, or holding onto something like a trolley, or carrying an umbrella. There are lots of different safety behaviours that people can engage in to try to help cope with the problem, and we will come to your safety behaviours a little later. Another coping strategy is *escape*. Many people with agoraphobia recount stories of when they abandoned their shopping trolley and quickly left the supermarket due to feelings of panic.

To sum up, there are a number of symptoms of agoraphobia: feelings (anxiety and panic); physical symptoms (palpitations etc.); thoughts ('I'm going to have a heart attack' etc.); and behaviours (avoidance – not going places for fear of feeling anxious; safety behaviours – doing things or taking things with you to help reduce anxiety; and escape – leaving a situation when feeling panicky).

Consequences of agoraphobia

Agoraphobia can at times feel like a mental prison that limits your life. It may also have a number of consequences for your daily routines. You might have tried to overcome your agoraphobia before but not succeeded. It can be incredibly difficult! Loved ones may have offered you well-meaning advice that might not have helped, despite your best efforts to follow it. At this point, you might feel hopeless about your situation. Because of this, the book is written in several short sections that will allow you to address your agoraphobia one step at a time, at a pace that is manageable for you, and in a way that should allow you to overcome your agoraphobia and begin living your life to the full.

What is cognitive behavioural therapy?

This book is based on an evidence-based psychological therapeutic approach called cognitive behavioural therapy, or CBT for short. The evidence supporting this approach comes from many research trials which are summarised in important scientific reviews. These reviews say that CBT is effective for lots of people who experience anxiety difficulties (including agoraphobia) and also depression. Of course, sometimes people with an anxiety disorder will become depressed as well due to the consequences of experiencing long-term anxiety and this is not uncommon in agoraphobia.

CBT can be provided in a number of ways including: face-to-face with a therapist, by telephone or using online technology; in a group setting with others also living with agoraphobia; or in a self-help format such as provided by this book. Sometimes you can get support while using self-help from a healthcare professional. A family member or friend can also act as a supporter.

The use of CBT self-help books is often referred to as 'low-intensity CBT'. It's called 'low intensity' because there is a strong emphasis on the use of self-help materials rather than sessions with a therapist. It used to be thought that low-intensity CBT was only suitable for people with mild problems, but more recent research evidence supports this form of therapy for anyone suffering from anxiety and depression. This means, that no matter how severe or longstanding your agoraphobia is, this self-help book can help.

Using self-help

One of the advantages of self-help is that you can use the tools described within the book at a pace that best suits you. Saying that, similarly to taking a course of medicine, the approach works best if you keep going with it consistently rather than trying it for a bit, having a rest for a month and then picking it up again. Self-help is also an empowering approach in that you will know that the benefit you have gained has been through *your* own efforts.

You might have done some reading about your agoraphobia and come across CBT on the internet, so you may already be familiar with some of its principles. However, if this is your first experience of CBT self-help, flicking through this book may seem a bit daunting, which is completely understandable. You might worry about what lies ahead but do try not to.

How to use this book

The book is structured so that you can learn about your agoraphobia, consider goals that you want to achieve, begin to make changes, and learn how to maintain the gains you make and manage any setbacks. It can be difficult to tackle this kind of problem for all sorts of reasons, especially if it has been troubling you for a long time. Do try to bear this in mind as you work your way through the exercises in the book, so that you can be forgiving of yourself when times are tough. Remember that the benefits will repay your efforts.

There is no right or wrong way to use this book. Some people like to read through the entire book before going back to start tackling the problem. You might prefer to work through the sections of the book in order. Maybe you would prefer to dive straight in and use the techniques in Section 3. You might like to read first about how other people have used low-intensity CBT to help them overcome their agoraphobia to get a sense of what is expected before committing to doing it yourself (Section 5). Whatever you find to be the most helpful for you is absolutely fine. What is important is that you are ready to make a change that requires time and commitment.

It may be that a healthcare professional has recommended this self-help book to you and you are working through it together with them. If this is the case, they will be able to answer any questions that you might have, offer you additional advice and may even be able to coach you in completing the exercises. If you are working through the book on your own, you may find it useful to highlight helpful bits of text or add notes in the margins as you go along. If you are not sure about something, remember that another advantage of using a self-help book is that you can simply go back and read that section or paragraph again. If you need to do this, please don't become frustrated with or critical of yourself. It can feel like there is a lot to take in! What is most important is that you understand the techniques that are described within the book.

Sections of the book

The book is divided into five sections. Hopefully there will be something in each one that is relevant to you and helps you to tackle your agoraphobia. Here is an overview of what each section contains so that you know where to find what you are looking for.

Section 1: Getting going

Section 1 is about getting started and setting your own pace for working through the book. You'll find some top tips to increase your likelihood of success. Towards the end of this section you're encouraged to set some personal goals to help you track your progress. CBT self-help tends to work best if you can dedicate some time every day to tackling your problem, although this may not always be possible. That is fine too but do try to dedicate at least sixty to ninety minutes, three to five times a week. You will have to do this for a few weeks to reap the full benefits although you may well notice some early improvements, which will hopefully spur you on to keep going.

Section 2: Understanding agoraphobia

In this section we'll look at what agoraphobia is, including its symptoms, some potential causes and what keeps it going. We'll also look at panic disorder and its links to agoraphobia as many people say that this is how their agoraphobia started. In particular, this section aims to help you understand more about how your agoraphobia is affecting your ability to live your life the way that you want to, and what may be maintaining the problem. You will also learn how to break the vicious cycle of agoraphobia to help you start living the life you want to lead.

Section 3: Assessing the problem and using graded exposure to tackle it

This section first focuses on assessing your problem, then moves on to using CBT self-help to beat your agoraphobia using graded exposure. There will be space to think about what might have caused your agoraphobia, we'll look at ways of making sense of your symptoms and how they are interlinked, and consider what it is that is keeping your agoraphobia going. You will be supported to plan your own personal graded exposure plan to help you get on top of your agoraphobia. There is guidance for carrying out your plan and how to review the progress you make. There are also some tips on how to tackle any stumbling blocks you might encounter along the way.

Section 4: The relapse management toolkit

Here the focus is on what you can do to try to make sure that the changes you have made to your life are long-lasting and plan what to do if you experience a re-emergence of symptoms. If your agoraphobia is still significantly interfering with your life having worked through the book, we will look at what next steps you can take to address the problem. Low-intensity CBT has helped many people overcome their agoraphobia, and the majority of those people stay well. However, it is also natural to experience setbacks along the way. Therefore, the main focus of this section is showing you how to maintain the progress you have made and to look at ways of dealing with setbacks.

Section 5: Recovery stories

In the final section, you will be able to catch up with the people who are introduced in Section 2. Here, they share their stories of having agoraphobia and describe how they overcame their difficulties. You can see how they put their plans into action, what stumbling blocks they encountered along the way and how they continued to stay on top of their agoraphobia. Their stories will be different from yours, but you are likely to see some similarities. The techniques they used to tackle their difficulties are the same ones described in this book that are recommended to help you with your agoraphobia.

Top tips on using this book

Before beginning to understand your agoraphobia and how it affects you, here are some top tips about how to use this self-help book. Some of these apply to the use of self-help in general. The tips come from people who have benefited from CBT self-help to overcome their difficulties and from healthcare professionals who support people in using CBT self-help.

Top tip 1: Give it your best shot

'I had lived with agoraphobia for a long time and I wasn't sure that anything could help me. I felt terrified at the thought of going to busy places alone but, as I gave it a go, and despite it being hard at times, I stuck with it and now I'm free to go where I want, when I want!'

Let's be honest about this from the outset: it is unlikely that working your way through this book and trying out the techniques is going to be easy. There are likely to be challenges along the way. The techniques you will learn will mean that you will need to confront some situations that you have been avoiding, probably for a very long time. Be reassured that this will be done in a controlled and paced way. What is important is giving it your best shot and following the guidance on how to deal with the challenges and possible setbacks that come along. Reading through the stories of others who have used these techniques to tackle their agoraphobia may help (Section 5). If things ever seem like they are getting on top of you and you are thinking about giving up, turn to the troubleshooting guide in Section 3 (page 98). If a healthcare professional is supporting you, talk to them about things you are finding difficult. They will be able to check that you are using the techniques in a way that is likely to bring about the most benefit as well as offer encouragement and help troubleshooting difficulties.

Top tip 2: Put what you have learned into action

'What really helped was getting an understanding of what was keeping my agoraphobia going, then taking small steps towards tackling the problem by doing the exercises in the book. I wrote things down and recorded how I got on, which really helped motivate me to carry on.'

This is very much a 'doing' book rather than a 'reading' book. Putting what you learn into action is the key to overcoming agoraphobia. Remember, you don't need to do everything at once; that wouldn't be the best way to tackle the problem. Rather, take a step-by-step approach to your problem, working at a pace that suits you. There is no need to feel overloaded with too much to try and change too quickly. Generally speaking, the more effort you put into it, the greater you will benefit. In this way, after doing some reading, putting these techniques into action is the key to getting on top of your agoraphobia.

Think of it as being a bit like learning to drive a car. The instructor provides tuition to drive the car and it can feel difficult to put everything that is being learned into practice at first. It is only with repeated practice that the learner becomes more confident. Without investing time in putting into practice what is being taught, the learner is unlikely to make the progress needed to pass the driving test. Even after passing the driving test, the newly qualified driver must continue to practise what has been learned to become more proficient and to develop confidence in their ability. It takes time and effort and some 'going it alone' to get there. Like learning any new skill, it takes time and practice, and is worth the effort in the end. And remember, nobody learned to drive from reading a book alone!

Top tip 3: Writing in the book is allowed – in fact it is encouraged!

'I was a bit reluctant at first, but I was glad I wrote in the book. It was helpful to look back on my notes, especially when I was having a blip. It reminded me how I had overcome obstacles in the past, so I was able to do some of the same things I had done last time to help. Another good thing about it was that it helped me to see just how far I had come in a relatively short time given that I have been living with agoraphobia for years!'

Like me, you were probably told when you were younger that you should never write in books. This book is different: it is designed to be written in – and the more you do it, the better! Making notes helps learning as you can apply what you are reading to yourself and it makes it easier to find important points that are particularly relevant to you.

To make it easier for you to make notes, at different points throughout the book you will see a notebook and pen symbol as a prompt for you to make some notes if you wish. Remember, it can be handy to look back and see the progress that you are making. Sometimes it can be easy to forget!

Top tip 4: Like everyone, expect to have good days and bad days

'It was all going really well, then there was a day I was just feeling a bit out of sorts and a bit jittery, not sure why. I still went to the supermarket as planned though. When I was there, I bumped into someone I hadn't seen for years. It really threw me, and I felt trapped in a longwinded conversation catching up on the last five years. I made an excuse and dashed out, leaving my shopping behind. I came home and cried. It felt like all that effort had been for nothing. I almost gave up to be honest. But the next day, I pushed myself to get on with my plan and follow through with going back to the supermarket, which helped me get back on track. I'm so glad I did!'

Hopefully, after a few weeks of using this book, you will begin to notice an improvement in your agoraphobia. Nevertheless, like everyone going through this kind of process, you are likely to have ups and downs, and some days will feel easier than others. Don't be discouraged – this is normal. Try your best to keep on track with your plan and not let how you are feeling affect what you do.

Top tip 5: Expect setbacks – they're normal

'I was going great guns and was feeling so good about the progress I had made so quickly. Then the Covid-19 lockdown came, and I had to shield because of my condition. When I was eventually allowed to go back out, it felt like I was back to square one. In some ways I was, but I got back to where I was a lot more quickly than it had taken me the first time, thankfully. It was just one of those things and there was nothing I could do about it until lockdown ended.'

When trying the exercises in this book, hopefully everything will go smoothly for you. For lots of people this will be the case. However, it is normal to have the odd setback, and although it might sound strange, setbacks can be useful. That's why Section 4 looks at how to deal with setbacks and what you can do to try to stop a setback becoming a lapse, and a lapse becoming a relapse. This will be explained later so don't worry about that right now. What is key is not to lose heart.

Top tip 6: Act according to your goals rather than how you feel

'It was difficult at times and I kept on listening to the voice in my head saying, "You can't do this, it's too hard", and the feelings of anxiety were so strong at times. It was then that I found reminding myself of my goals kept me going. I put a reminder in my phone that would be there every day saying, "Remember your goals, keep going, you can do this." I was a bit sceptical at first but looking back, it helped me feel like I could do it no matter what.'

A main focus of the book is to act according to your goals rather than how you think or feel. In fact, this book will ask you, in a graded and controlled way, to behave in the opposite way of your 'default setting' that has been established (possibly over a long time) because of your feelings of anxiety. With this in mind, you will be asked to set some goals a little later in this section. You will read more about the patterns of behaviour that maintain your agoraphobia and how to break these patterns in Sections 2 and 3. These insights are key to starting to get on top of your agoraphobia.

So, try not to listen to your thoughts when they are telling you that you can't do this or to your body when you become anxious. Try not to let manageable levels of anxiety stop you from either completing the exercises in this book or doing things that you need or want to do. For example, most of us have experienced some anxiety or fear going to the dentist or when taking an exam. Think how it would negatively impact our lives if we always avoided these kinds of situations.

Top tip 7: Let your doctor know that you are going to use this book

'I went to my doctor and showed her the book and told her about my plans to work through it. Bry, my partner, came with me so he was able to tell her how he planned to support me with it. She seemed pleased that I was doing something about my problem and asked me to go back in a month to check in on how I was doing. She seemed hopeful that doing this would work but said she could refer me to someone if I was finding it too difficult. I found it helpful to know that not everything was riding on the book and that I could get more help if needed.'

There should be no medical reason to stop you from using the techniques in this book. However, the exercises will ask you to do things that are likely to lead to a certain level of discomfort. It is also important to be aware that medications prescribed for psychological problems (as well as other substances such as caffeine, alcohol and some over-the-counter medications) can have an impact on how you react. For this reason, it is recommended that you make your doctor aware before engaging with the exercises recommended in Section 3 to talk through how this might be best managed.

Top tip 8: Involve family and friends if you can

'My partner Yasmin has been living with my problem too for years as it has impacted on the way she lives her life. She is delighted that I am finally doing something about it, in fact she's read the book and wants to support me working through it. She said the book helped her understand what it's like for me as well as learning what she can do to help.'

There are many ways that involving family and/or friends can be useful, providing of course that they are supportive. Don't pick someone who is going to be impatient or critical of you. In fact, even the process of telling loved ones that you have decided to work through this book to tackle your agoraphobia can make it more likely that you will carry it through.

Top tip 9: Set aside time to use the book and use reminders

'I wrote in my calendar to remind me every day to do an exercise from the book to help me with my agoraphobia. I don't think I would have forgotten, but it was a good prompt for me to get on and just do it.'

Some people report struggling to make time or forgetting to carry out their exercises because of other distractions. It is also not uncommon for people to put off the exercises because they feel they're too difficult or they don't feel like they want to experience the discomfort at that time. Putting it off is normal and is sometimes referred to as 'procrastination'. With this in mind, do consider setting reminders to help you follow through with the exercises.

Working on your agoraphobia may involve some planning and perhaps involve moving things around in your day but this will just be for a few weeks while you are working through the book. This is another reason to involve others (top tip 8). It might be that someone who is supporting you can help by taking over a commitment temporarily to allow you to have some additional time to focus on practising new ways of dealing with your agoraphobia. Incorporate time to focus on tackling your agoraphobia into your daily schedule. You could even start now by setting some time aside in your diary over the next few days to allow you to continue reading this book.

Using support

Self-help books such as this can be more effective when they are used with someone to support you. This makes sense. We are much more likely to turn up to a fitness class if we have arranged to meet a friend than if we have not. Equally, we are more likely to hand in work if we have committed to a deadline. There are several reasons for this. First, there is social pressure: if you know that someone is going to ask you how you got on with a particular exercise in this book, you are more likely to do the exercise. Second, other people sometimes have good ideas! They can help you if something doesn't make sense, and can also help you to make the exercises personally meaningful and relevant. Third, it's good to have people to support you and cheer you on.

For all of these reasons, you are encouraged to find a 'supporter': someone to help you work through this book and share your journey of recovery. Choose someone who you trust and see regularly, and with whom you feel you can be completely honest.

Getting professional support

If you don't have someone in your life who can be a supporter, or if you decide that you are uncomfortable bringing someone on board, then you could find a mental healthcare professional to help you. Your doctor may have information available on who could do this and how you can contact them, so talk to them if you think this might be something you would like to pursue.

Sometimes, people come a bit unstuck because they try to do too much at once. Getting off to a fast start doesn't necessarily make you first to cross the finish line. Remember the story of the tortoise and the hare! If you keep working on the problem, taking a step-by-step approach, you will reach where you want to be. It doesn't matter how long it takes; do it at your pace. You will know what pace is right for you – trust yourself!

It may be that you are already receiving support from your GP or another healthcare professional. In England, there are NHS Talking Therapies services where people can be supported to work through psychological problems by telephone, face-to-face or online. Psychological Wellbeing Practitioners (PWPs) are healthcare workers specifically trained to assess and support people in using self-help material such as this book.

Wherever you are in the world, it is worth speaking to your doctor to find out whether such a service exists and whether you can access it. What you can expect from this kind of service includes:

- Support sessions (this could be by telephone, face-to-face, in a group, or even by email or other technology).

- Guidance in completing the tasks in this book.

- Help to identify and solve any problems that you might encounter along the way.

- Answers to questions you might have.

A professional supporter such as this will also be able to guide you in how to get help if your problems do not improve. In England, to find out more about this kind of support visit www.nhs.uk and search for 'psychological therapy services'. You can usually self-refer, or you can ask your doctor to refer you.

You may not be receiving support in using this book, or you may live in an area where this kind of support is not available. If you feel that you need professional support, talk to your doctor who is likely to be able to refer you to or give you informa-tion about services that can offer a similar service.

However, there is also absolutely no reason why you can't use this book on your own, and many people find books such as this helpful without someone else's input. It may be that you want to be able to try out the different techniques and exercises at your own pace, or that you just prefer to tackle your problems by yourself. It's up to each of us to find what works best, and I hope this book will help you however you decide to use it. Please just keep in mind that professional support should be available if you need it. In some cases professional support will make it more likely that a person will be able to complete self-help.

Remember, there are no rules about how quickly you should move through this book. In fact, it is better to take things steadily and have repeated experiences of success, rather than move on too quickly to the next exercise; try to consolidate your learning on one step before moving to the next. There are no definite expectations around the amount of time it will take for you to complete it. This will depend on the time you are able to invest but, for the book to really help, I would ask you to commit to just two things:

1. Give it a go: read it and try it!

Give the exercises a go and see what works for you. The more that you put things into practice, the more likely it is you will reap the rewards. Remember that we all have days when we feel like giving up. Make a commitment to use the book and put the advice into practice, even if you are uncertain that it will work for you before you give it a try. Consider making a deal with yourself to give it your best shot for six weeks and see how you feel after that.

2. If things get really bad and you think about ending your life, speak to someone straightaway

For a few people, when they are experiencing emotional difficulties and things begin to get on top of them, they can feel so bad that they think about ending their life. If things get so bad that you are having these types of thoughts regularly and/or plan to harm yourself in any way, get help! There are details of support agencies listed in the back of this book (pages 198–200), some of which you can contact twenty-four hours a day. Let your doctor or other healthcare professional know how you feel. They can help. Tell someone else, such as a trusted friend or family member. They may be able to support you in getting help. Remember that you won't always feel this way and that there are things that you can do to help you feel better.

Feeling suicidal at times tends to be closely linked to the experience of hopelessness or depression. It is perhaps not surprising that when people have been living with agoraphobia for a long time, they can feel they don't want to carry on. Hopelessness and depression can be treated directly or can shift as you make progress towards your goals. When people recover in this way, they no longer feel like ending their life. If you frequently feel depressed, it can be a good idea to seek treatment for your depression first and then, when you are feeling brighter, you will be better placed to start working through this book. If what is written in this paragraph reflects how you are feeling, it is important to discuss this with your doctor.

Making change happen

Many people, who would otherwise struggle to get going with making the changes necessary to tackle their problems, have found the following exercise to be helpful as it really focuses the mind. Please complete the questions in the box below to think about change. You can write as much or as little as you like. Afterwards, I'll help you to set goals that you want to work on.

How important is it for me to change?

Write down all of the ways that your problem has limited your life to date. Additionally, describe how your problem might impact your life in the future if it remains the same or even worsens. How will it interfere with you achieving your life goals? What have you had to sacrifice for this problem? Imagine that you go to sleep tonight, and you wake up tomorrow and everything in your life is how you want it to be with agoraphobia no longer being a problem for you. Use the space below to write what your life would look like if this happened.

....

....

....

....

....

....

Do I have the opportunity to change?

Imagine that working through this book and all its exercises will take around sixty to ninety minutes a day, for three to five days a week (every day if possible), for twelve weeks. To be able to prioritise your work on the problem for these three months, what needs to change in your life? Are there some commitments that you can do less often? Is there some extra support that you can enlist temporarily? Do you remember what was mentioned earlier about calendar reminders? Write down what you can put in place to allow you to give yourself the best chance of completing this self-help.

....

....

....

....

....

Thinking ahead

You've now considered what your life would look like if it was no longer affected by agoraphobia and the time commitment needed to make those changes. Now let's think about the process of achieving your goal to get the life you want. The way to do this is to break things down into more manageable and focused goals that you would like to achieve over the next few months. These goals may be the things that you used to do but have had to stop doing because of your agoraphobia, or it could be new things that you would like to do in the future that are currently not possible.

Setting goals is a great way to identify exactly what you want to achieve by putting into practice the strategies you are going to learn over the following chapters. The best goals are:

- Specific

- Measurable

- Achievable

- Realistic

- Time-bound.

The acronym for remembering these characteristics is SMART. Setting goals this way can really help when it comes to maintaining a focus on where you want to be, which in turn will enable you to assess your progress. Try to avoid goals like 'I want to feel normal again'. This is a very understandable and reasonable goal. It is also a realistic goal. However, it isn't particularly 'SMART' as it is very general and so less measurable.

Making your goals SMART will help ensure that you achieve them. Being specific about what you are setting out to achieve means that you will know where to begin to try to achieve it. If you have a goal that is not measurable, you won't know if you've met it or not. If your goal is not achievable and realistic, it may end up feeling like something you've failed at, and that is never pleasant. If it is not time-limited, then you risk losing interest and focus. Let's look in more detail at how to make your goals SMART:

1. Specific. Rather than setting a goal 'to be able to go wherever I like', think about what in particular is missing from your life that means you are not able to go wherever you like and that you want to reintroduce. For instance, you might want to 'go on my own to the supermarket at busy times at least once a week, leaving only when my shopping is complete'. That is likely to be a pretty useful goal for someone who is struggling to go shopping.

2. Measurable. Being able to go wherever you like is quite difficult to measure as it is so broad and some places might be more difficult than others, but you can easily determine whether or not you are going to the supermarket on your own at busy times once a week.

3. Achievable. Being able to go wherever you like should be achievable, but having more clearly defined goals that specify exactly what you would like to achieve is more helpful. Think about what you would like to achieve by the end of this book (say, three months). Going to the supermarket, cinema, department store or theatre, and using public transport alone should all be achievable if you are able to put in the time and effort to get there.

4. Realistic. Someone might set a goal of flying to Australia on their own without experiencing any fear. Realistically, that is unlikely to be something that most people will be able to do in three months for practical reasons alone. It is not that flying to Australia is not important or even achievable, but it is probably not as helpful as a goal that can be just as challenging but can be done every week. Try to keep it reasonably local and something that is currently limiting your lifestyle in some meaningful way, such as being able to go to the shops or using public transport. Mastering situations like this can have the most meaningful impact on your life as well as help you reach the global stuff.

5. Time-bound. Try to ensure that your goals are achievable within the timeframe. 'I want to give my daughter away at her wedding' is not an ideal goal if your daughter is only seven! Stay in the here and now and aim for what you want to be able to do in three months' time.

When you have decided on the goals that you would like to achieve, rate each one in respect of how far you can achieve the goal right now. The idea is for you to come back and re-rate your goals in one, two and three months' time to measure your progress.

My goals for overcoming my agoraphobia

Goal 1: ....

....

....

I can do this now   (Today's date___/___/___)
(circle a number):

0	1	2	3	4	5	6
Not at all		Occasionally		Often		Any time

One-month re-rating   (date___/___/___)
(circle a number):

0	1	2	3	4	5	6
Not at all		Occasionally		Often		Any time

Two-month re-rating   (date___/___/___)
(circle a number):

0	1	2	3	4	5	6
Not at all		Occasionally		Often		Any time

Three-month re-rating   (date___/___/___)
(circle a number):

0	1	2	3	4	5	6
Not at all		Occasionally		Often		Any time

Goal 2: ....

....

....

I can do this now   (Today's date___/___/___)
(circle a number):

0	1	2	3	4	5	6
Not at all		Occasionally		Often		Any time

One-month re-rating   (date___/___/___)
(circle a number):

0	1	2	3	4	5	6
Not at all		Occasionally		Often		Any time

Two-month re-rating   (date___/___/___)
(circle a number):

0	1	2	3	4	5	6
Not at all		Occasionally		Often		Any time

Three-month re-rating   (date___/___/___)
(circle a number):

   0   1   2   3   4   5   6
Not at all   Occasionally   Often   Any time

Goal 3: ....

....

....

I can do this now   (Today's date___/___/___)
(circle a number):

   0   1   2   3   4   5   6
Not at all   Occasionally   Often   Any time

One-month re-rating   (date___/___/___)
(circle a number):

   0   1   2   3   4   5   6
Not at all   Occasionally   Often   Any time

Two-month re-rating   (date___/___/___)
(circle a number):

   0   1   2   3   4   5   6
Not at all   Occasionally   Often   Any time

Three-month re-rating   (date___/___/___)
(circle a number):

0   1   2   3   4   5   6
Not at all   Occasionally   Often   Any time

If you have read this section and followed the exercises, you will have considered what your life will be like if you can make changes. You will also have set some relevant goals for going forward. Now let's keep going. Earlier, you were encouraged to make some plans regarding how you are going to schedule in time to begin working on your problem. If you did that, great; if not, try to do that now.

Hopefully you are feeling motivated and ready to start. In Section 2, we'll look at how to make sense of agoraphobia, which will lead us nicely on to looking at how to overcome it in Section 3. Let's go!

UNDERSTANDING AGORAPHOBIA

People with agoraphobia often ask themselves questions like:

'What is agoraphobia?'

'What is fight or flight?'

'How common is agoraphobia?'

'What caused my agoraphobia?'

'How has it managed to take over my whole life?'

'How can I overcome it?'

'Is it possible to overcome agoraphobia if you've had it for a long time?'

'If I overcome it, will it come back?'

In this section, we're going to look at key information about agoraphobia and answer all these questions, and hopefully any others that you might have. We'll then move on to look at the ways agoraphobia is affecting your life.

Often people request help for a psychological problem because of:

- How they **feel** ('I feel frightened'). Feelings, whether positive or negative, are usually described in one word (for example: 'panicky', 'depressed', 'anxious' etc.).

- **Physical** symptoms occurring in their body ('my heart is pounding, 'my chest is tight', etc.).

- Patterns in their **thinking** ('sometimes I think I can't carry on like this', 'this is not the life I want to live', etc.).

- Changes in their lifestyle or **behaviour**, including what extra they have had to do to cope ('I'm comfort eating') or what they can't do any more ('I can't get the bus to work').

The model of CBT that we are going to use assumes that feelings, thoughts, physical symptoms and behaviours are all connected and affect each other. Making sense of agoraphobia is helped by understanding how these connections work.

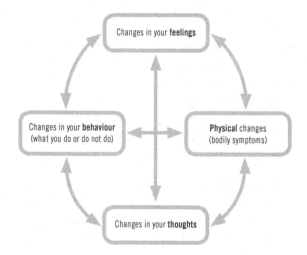

While the impact of agoraphobia will affect each of these symptom areas in a similar way, your symptoms will be different from those of other people, and unique to you.

In this section you will learn about Zoe and Haider, and we will catch up with them again in Section 5. Hopefully, some of their experiences will be relevant to you. Over the course of the book, the idea is that their experiences will give you some insight into:

- The connections between symptom areas.

- Some of the challenges faced by people who experience agoraphobia.

- How challenges can be overcome.

Stories of people with agoraphobia

It's time to introduce you to Zoe and Haider who have shared their experiences of having lived with agoraphobia for a long time and how they got on using CBT self-help.

Zoe

Zoe is a thirty-two-year-old married woman who has one child aged four years. Her main difficulty is a fear of panicking in public places and collapsing. Her problems started in her early twenties when she had a panic attack on a bus. The next time she tried to go on a bus she felt anxious and came home. She tried a few more times but did not manage to get on a bus. Since then she avoided all public transport but overcame travelling difficulties by learning to drive (except on motorways).

After the birth of her son four years ago, Zoe's agoraphobia worsened. She generally felt more anxious, and when her son was six months old she had a panic attack while driving. She rang her husband who picked her up and took her home, but after that she avoided driving altogether. Zoe also started to feel anxious in large shopping centres and supermarkets, and started to avoid them too.

Zoe decided to do something about her agoraphobia because she was worried that her problem would get so bad that she would be unable to get out of the house. She was also worried that she would not be able to take her son to school. Zoe was depressed, with a loss of interest in previously enjoyed activities (such as reading, watching television and making specialist cakes).

Zoe experienced the following symptoms:

Feelings – 'Anxiety and panic.'

Physical – 'When I feel anxious, I get "butterflies" in my stomach, a racing heart and feel hot and sweaty, and when I panic these feelings become much worse and intense and I feel everything closing in on me.'

Thoughts – 'During a panic I think I will collapse and die.'

Behaviour – 'I avoid all forms of public transport, driving, large shops, supermarkets, shopping centres and queues. If I can, I avoid going out altogether.'

Zoe always found things easier if she was with her friend or husband and that pushing her son's push-chair helped (these serving as safety behaviours). Zoe enlisted the help of her husband and friend as supporters, and together with them decided on the following goals:

Goal 1. Go to the supermarket three times a week and stay for at least one hour.

Goal 2. Drive to my parents' house an hour away (using the motorway) once a week.

Goal 3. Travel by train (one hour each way) alone every two weeks.

Haider

Haider is a fifty-four-year-old single man who lives alone. He has been living with agoraphobia for nearly thirty years. His main difficulty is leaving the house unaccompanied for fear of having a heart attack. His problems started in his mid-twenties after a long illness (not related to his heart) that required a fairly lengthy stay in hospital and several weeks convalescing at home. When he was eventually well enough to leave home, he became intensely anxious and experienced chest pain with a racing heart. The next time he tried to go out, the symptoms were the same and he stayed at home instead. His fear of going out has continued and worsened over the years.

Haider does all his shopping online, although his mum pops round most days to check he is alright and to drop off some groceries. His close friend takes him to the cinema twice a month where he sits near the exit at the end of a row so that he can leave quickly if he feels anxiety symptoms coming on. He leaves before the credits to avoid the rush. Haider works from home and decided to do something about his agoraphobia as he was tired of his life being so restricted and wanted to find a job that would be better paid, but felt unable to apply for any jobs due to his difficulties in going out.

Haider experienced the following symptoms:

Feelings – 'Fear and panic.'

Physical – 'When I feel anxious, I get a racing heart, chest pain, light-headedness and feel unsteady, and when I panic these feelings become much worse and intense and I feel like I'm going to die.'

Thoughts – 'I'm going to have a heart attack.'

Behaviour – 'I avoid going out unless I am with someone. I manage to go to the cinema but only with my friend and have to make sure I can leave quickly if I feel panicky. I have not been in a shop or used public transport for years. I pretty much avoid going out altogether if I can.'

Haider always found it easier if he was with his friend or mum and would usually take a walking stick to lean on in case he felt lightheaded or unsteady (which served as a safety behaviour). Initially, Haider decided to work on his problem alone but later enlisted the help of his friend and mum as supporters. Haider's goals were to:

Goal 1. Walk alone to the local shopping precinct four times a week and stay for at least one hour.

Goal 2. Go to the cinema alone once a week, sitting in the middle of a row far from the exit and leaving the same time as everyone else.

Goal 3. Travel by bus for at least an hour on my own once a week.

The personal circumstances of Zoe and Haider, their ages and lifestyles, are likely to be different from your own. However, the techniques that they used to help them to overcome their agoraphobia are the same as the ones that should help you. In Section 5, you can read their full stories and how they used CBT self-help to enable them to make changes to their lives. You will find out what went well and about some of the challenges that they met along the way, and what they did to overcome them. It may not always be easy for you either, but reading about others' experiences and the challenges they faced and overcame can help you keep on track.

Questions and answers

Zoe and Haider's stories show how people can experience agoraphobia very differently. However, you are likely to still have questions about agoraphobia and why this has happened to you. Next, you'll find answers to some of the most common questions people ask.

Question 1: What is agoraphobia?

Agoraphobia is an anxiety disorder. It is a fear of being in situations where escape might be difficult or where you believe that help wouldn't be available if something went wrong.

To be formally diagnosed with agoraphobia, you will have experienced marked fear or anxiety about two or more of the following five 'problem areas' for six months or longer. Tick those situations that apply to you.

Problem Area	Situation	Tick if applies to you
Transport such as:	Driving a car	
	Using the bus or tram	
	Travelling by train	
	Using the Underground	
	Travelling by boat/ship	
	Travelling by aeroplane	
Open spaces such as:	Car parks	
	Market places	
Enclosed spaces such as:	Shops	
	Supermarkets	
	Department stores	
	Theatres	
	Cinemas	
Standing in a queue		
Being in a crowd		
Being away from home alone		

Do your goals reflect your problem areas? If not, consider revising your goals so that you are targeting a problem area listed here or even add in another goal.

Here is a bit more detail about agoraphobia diagnosis:

- You will fear or avoid the situations you ticked in the table because of thoughts that either escape might be difficult or help might not be available if you experience feelings of panic or display troubling or embarrassing behaviours such as screaming, crying uncontrollably or feeling unable to stand without falling over.

- You will find that the situations you ticked in the table almost always cause you fear or anxiety and you will avoid them altogether or need someone to be with you. You might be able to endure them at times but not without intense fear or anxiety.

- The fear or anxiety is out of proportion to the actual danger. For instance, it is not actually dangerous to go to the supermarket or travel by public transport.

- You will have found that avoiding these situations has had a significant impact on various areas of your life. For instance, your social life, work and perhaps other aspects of your day-to-day living will be affected.

Agoraphobia can be a problem in its own right although some people also have panic disorder. If

your symptoms meet the criteria for both agoraphobia and panic disorder you would usually be
considered to have both. So, let's now look at panic
disorder as it is likely to be just as relevant to you.

Panic disorder

Panic disorder is closely linked to agoraphobia. To
be formally diagnosed with panic disorder, you will
experience recurrent and unexpected panic attacks.
Panic attacks are sudden surges of intense fear or
discomfort that reach a peak within minutes and
can feel like they have 'come out of the blue'.

To be formally diagnosed with panic disorder, you
will experience four or more of the following symptoms. Tick those symptoms that apply to you.

Symptoms	Tick if applies to you
Palpitations, heart pounding/racing	
Sweating	
Trembling or shaking	
Shortness of breath or feeling of being smothered	
Choking sensation	

Chest pain	
Feeling sick	
Tummy upset or discomfort	
Dizziness, light-headedness, feeling unsteady or faint	
Feeling chills or heat sensations	
Numbness or tingling	
Feelings of unreality or like you are detached from yourself	
Fear of losing control or 'going mad'	
Fear that you are going to die	

Further, if you have panic disorder, you will find that you will have experienced one or both of the following for at least a month:

1. Worry about having another panic attack and what might happen (e.g. 'I'll faint', 'I'll have a heart attack', 'I'll go mad').

2. A big change in your behaviour so as to avoid future panic attacks (e.g. stopping exercising or travelling by public transport etc.).

It might be that your agoraphobia started with panic disorder. This is very common. You might no longer experience panic attacks through avoidance of agoraphobia symptoms but may fear having panic attacks when entering those situations. If you decide that your problem is panic disorder rather than agoraphobia, you may prefer to work through a self-help book directly about panic or panic disorder.

Some useful information about agoraphobia and panic disorder is available on the UK's NHS website. At time of writing, the direct links are:

https://www.nhs.uk/conditions/agoraphobia/

https://www.nhs.uk/conditions/panic-disorder/

Question 2: What is fight or flight?

Anxiety is a normal emotion and an important part of life as it acts as a basic survival mechanism, commonly known as 'fight or flight'. You may have heard of it. This is our body's primitive, inborn, automatic response that helps us prepare to confront danger by either facing it head on ('fight') or running away ('flight'). There are many everyday situations where it is reasonable to experience some degree of anxiety. For example, if you are about to cross a busy road where there is no pedestrian crossing, it is realistic to feel a little anxious about potentially getting hit by a vehicle. In this scenario, anxiety helps you to keep vigilant and pay more attention to the traffic, thereby keeping you safe. However, for some people, anxiety happens too frequently (when they are not faced with real danger), it is too intense (it leads to panic attacks) or lasts too long (it goes on longer than the stressful situation). So, although anxiety is normal and vital to our survival, in certain circumstances it can be unhelpful and debilitating. This is the case with agoraphobia.

Having an understanding of the fight-or-flight response and being able to make sense of bodily sensations as symptoms of anxiety, rather than something more sinister, can be extremely helpful.

Question 3: How common is agoraphobia?

Agoraphobia affects 1–3 per cent of the population and it is twice as common in women as it is men. Agoraphobia usually begins in young adulthood between the ages of eighteen and thirty-five.

Question 4: What causes agoraphobia?

There are lots of different explanations as to why people develop agoraphobia. Some theories suggest that there is a genetic link (i.e. inherited), while others advocate that life events (such as bereavement or other traumatic event) may be the trigger for agoraphobia. Another idea is that it is caused by an imbalance of chemicals in the brain.

Most people will develop agoraphobia as a complication of panic disorder. For instance, agoraphobia often develops if a person has a panic attack for no apparent reason (it came 'out of the blue') in a public place. The person begins to worry about having another panic attack and associates the panic and/or anxiety with going to public places and can start to feel the symptoms of panic coming back when they're in a similar situation again. This leads the person to avoid that particular situation as they learn that avoidance relieves anxiety. Thus, an association develops between going out and panic attacks.

Not everyone can pinpoint a cause to the development of their agoraphobia though. It may be due to a combination of factors rather than one alone, but most cases of agoraphobia do develop as a complication of panic disorder. Importantly, whether you know the cause or not, this has no bearing on the success of the techniques in this book.

Lots of people like to have some understanding of why their problems started, so you might want to try to do that. Use the box provided to write down your ideas about why you think your agoraphobia started and what factors are keeping it going.

1. What I think started my agoraphobia

....

....

....

....

....

....

....

....

2. What I think is keeping my agoraphobia going

....

....

....

....

....

....

....

....

Agoraphobia without panic disorder

Sometimes, and less commonly, a person can develop agoraphobia without a history of panic disorder or panic attacks.

This type of agoraphobia can be triggered by a number of different irrational fears or phobias such as the fear of:

- Becoming a victim of a violent crime or a terrorist attack if leaving home.

- Becoming infected by a serious illness if visiting crowded places.

- Accidentally doing something that will result in embarrassment or humiliation in front of other people.

Question 5: Why can having agoraphobia feel like it has taken over a person's whole life?

You might remember reading in Section 1 how avoidance may seem quite natural to you in situations where your agoraphobia has an effect on you. This is because fears and anxieties can grow and turn into agoraphobia through a vicious cycle involving avoidance. Look at Zoe's experience of trying to go to the supermarket.

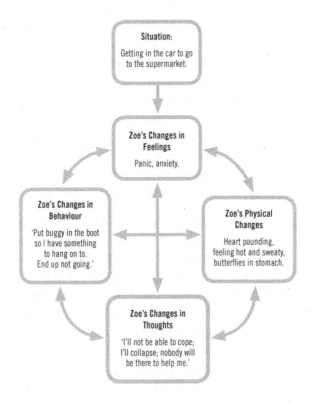

This diagram shows how the symptoms affect each other to heighten anxiety and impact on a person's life. In response to fear and anxiety, people can experience the unpleasant physical symptoms associated with the fight-or-flight response (such as sweating and heart racing) which can, in turn, lead to thoughts focusing on threat ('I'm going to have a heart attack', 'I'm going to faint'). Sometimes people are mostly unaware of these kinds of thoughts and are more aware of the unpleasant physical symptoms instead. In either case, the unpleasant symptoms can be taken to confirm the presence of threat ('Because I am anxious, I am in danger of something bad happening'), and the natural thing to do is avoid the thing that triggers this experience (e.g. the supermarket). This provides a powerful sense of relief, which means the person is more likely to do the same again when faced with similar circumstances.

The frustrating thing about avoidance and escape is that it removes the opportunity for the person to find out that nothing bad will happen and that they can learn more helpful ways of coping with the fear. As such, they get a bit stuck. Imagine a situation where a child thinks there's a monster living in their wardrobe. If they never open the door to check, they never discover that it is just in their imagination! Avoidance is the powerful maintaining influence of the vicious circle as it denies the person the opportunity to move forward.

Above and beyond this, once a person starts to avoid, there is a natural process that is called 'generalisation', where situations that share similar features with the original situation or environment are avoided as well. So, if a person originally avoids one particular supermarket, they might begin to avoid all supermarkets, shops and department stores. In this way, fear and anxiety grows through avoidance behaviour and generalisation. As they grow, they tend to affect more and more aspects of the person's life.

Question 6: What can be done to overcome agoraphobia?

The good news is that low-intensity CBT has been shown to work for people who use it. CBT is a very structured and practical approach that lends itself well to a low-intensity self-help format. It involves using self-help material such as this book, which provides information about the same techniques that you would use if you were seeing a healthcare professional for face-to-face sessions. As mentioned earlier, this approach can be used without any support from a professional, but having support can be beneficial for many people, especially if maintaining motivation is a struggle. Friends and family can offer support too of course, and you are advised to recruit a trusted person as a supporter if you can.

Question 7: Is it possible to overcome agoraphobia if you've had it for a long time?

The short and honest answer to this question is yes! Agoraphobia is actually a very treatable problem.

However, many people find it very difficult to overcome. This is generally because they think the best way to overcome it is to first find a way to get rid of their fears, and then re-enter the situations they came to avoid. Unfortunately, this is the wrong way round, and it is by re-entering the situations in a specific manner (see Section 3) that leads to a reduction in fears. Lots of people live with agoraphobia for many years before mustering up the courage to do something about it. Whether you have had the problem for one year or forty years, the tried-and-tested strategies in this book can help. There is no reason to be less ambitious with your goals either. Think about what you would like to be able to do and let's go for it!

Question 8: Will it come back?

Good news! Of those people who are treated for anxiety disorders, the majority will stay well. The flipside of course is that there will be some people who will experience anxiety symptoms again in the future. There is no agreed way of predicting who will relapse and who will not. What we do know is that people who are able to spot early warning signs that symptoms may be returning tend to do better. This awareness allows them to put the techniques that previously worked for them into practice again to stop these early signs of lapse becoming a full-blown relapse (information on what setbacks, lapse and relapse are can be found in Section 4). Remember too that everyone will experience fear and anxiety at times. This is a natural protective response to threat. So, it is really important not to misinterpret normal experiences of anxiety as being a problem.

In Section 4, you will read about the 'relapse management toolkit'. Should you begin to experience early warning signs of your agoraphobia returning (for instance, if you start to have an urge to avoid going to the shops), you can use the toolkit to act on this setback to help avoid a relapse.

Although it's not possible to guarantee that you'll not experience a return of your symptoms in the future, the tools and techniques in this book will help equip you to get on top of the problem again. These are lifelong skills to help you to take control of your agoraphobia. Rather than try to avoid experiencing your agoraphobia again, it is much more helpful to keep an eye out for early warning signs that indicate to you (or others who are close to you) that there are signs of it returning.

How does your agoraphobia affect you?

So far, we've looked at how your agoraphobia:

- Is generally experienced emotionally (feelings).

- Is likely to affect you physically.

- Will affect your thoughts.

- Will affect what you do (or don't do).

Now let's try to apply this understanding to your situation using the same diagram as used for Zoe earlier in this section. As a further demonstration of how this works, on the opposite page you can see how symptoms relate to each other for Haider when he's confronted with going out of the house alone.

Using Haider's example opposite, fill in the areas of the blank diagram (on page 65) to list the symptoms triggered by one of your agoraphobic situations (it can help to use a recent example of when it happened to you, so it is clearer in your mind).

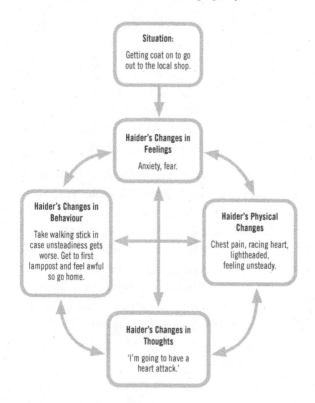

1. What was the *situation*?

2. What were the *feelings* you experienced when confronted with your feared situation? Write these in the 'feelings' box.

3. What *physical* changes in your body did you notice when confronted with your feared

situation? Write these in the box labelled 'physical changes'.

4. Now consider what *thoughts* were going through your mind at the time. Add these into the 'thoughts' box. These are likely to be focused on some form of threat like Haider's thoughts (e.g. 'I am going to have a heart attack').

5. Next, think about how feeling this way affected how you behaved. In the 'behaviour' box, make a note of the things that you did. In particular think about *avoidance*, *escape* and *safety behaviours*. For example, deciding not to go (avoidance); leaving the situation before you are finished (escape); drinking more alcohol; taking a bottle or water with you; having medication in your pocket; holding onto something; asking someone to go with you etc. (safety behaviours).

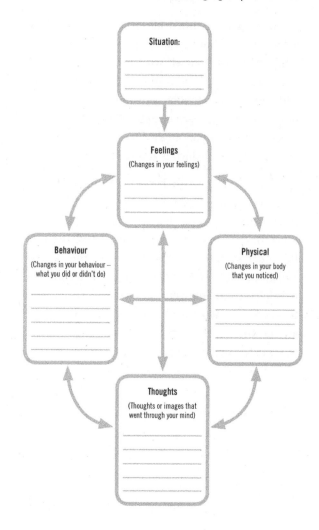

Once you have finished filling in the boxes, have a look to see how symptoms interact with each other. Also, ask yourself whether this is typical of your agoraphobia. You could do the diagram again with another agoraphobic situation to check. You'll probably find that each symptom interacts with the others, although you might find that some arrows are one way only, which is absolutely fine too.

As mentioned, agoraphobia is maintained through avoidance, escape and safety behaviours. Changing these behaviours can effectively break the vicious cycle. In changing your behaviour, it will affect all the other symptoms. This then turns into a new 'positive cycle' (see next diagram) as the techniques to help you to change your behaviours reduce symptoms and help to increase confidence. As you move around the positive cycle again and again, you are likely to feel better and better.

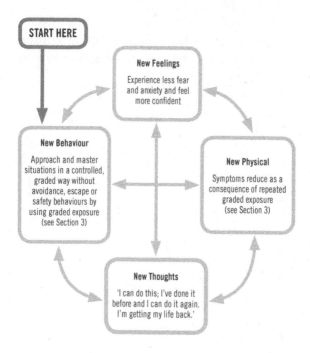

Just as it took time for your vicious cycle to develop, it is likely to take time to reverse it and turn it into a positive cycle. This book aims to show you the steps that you can take to make this happen. The biggest step is getting to the stage where you are feeling ready to make the change. You will also hopefully have thought about some goals to aim towards and the timescale for reaching them. You are now ready to move on to Section 3 where we shall look at how you can break this cycle and begin to make the changes to your life that are going to make it so much better.

ASSESSING THE PROBLEM AND USING GRADED EXPOSURE TO TACKLE IT

If you have completed reading and doing the exercises in Sections 1 and 2, great! Hopefully you've found the information about agoraphobia to be useful. You are likely to have seen aspects of your own agoraphobia reflected in what you have read so far. It's good you've stayed with it and I hope you are reassured that there is a tried-and-tested way forward to tackle your agoraphobia.

If your symptoms have a different pattern from those described in the last section, it may be that you have a different type of problem. If this is the case, and if you have not done so already, it would be worthwhile talking to your doctor or other healthcare professional before continuing further with the book. There are a variety of anxiety problems. Agoraphobia is just one of them.

If you've turned straight to this section because either you want to get going with tackling your problem straightaway or you know about agoraphobia already, welcome! By way of a brief recap, this is what we've spent time looking at so far:

- Symptoms and goals (Section 1).

- Factors that influence the development of agoraphobia (Section 2).

- The vicious cycle of avoidance, escape and safety behaviours that keeps agoraphobia going (Section 2).

In terms of your own symptoms, you were able to compare them to those experienced by Zoe and Haider, our case examples. If you haven't completed this exercise, please turn back to page 65 and fill in your symptoms in the diagram as these will be your target for trying out the techniques described in this section. It would also be helpful if you could have a look at the vicious cycle of avoidance (pages 63–68). You may also want to complete your goals for treatment (pages 35–8); these are important as they give you something to aim for and allow you to monitor your progress.

Now it's time to break into the vicious cycle of behaviours that are maintaining your agoraphobia.

In this section, we are going to get you started in overcoming your agoraphobia by using 'graded exposure'. This is an intervention that is part of CBT (the psychological therapy described on page 6). Here, you will learn about graded exposure and how it works, then move on to making a plan to put graded exposure into action.

Key points

Remember that you are in charge of what you do to tackle your agoraphobia. If you are not clear about something, do go back to re-read the relevant parts of the book. You can look over your notes and any text you have high-lighted. Do please keep on making notes and highlighting as you go. The key thing is to use this book to apply graded exposure and put it into action to change your life. Unfortunately, reading the book alone without doing the graded exposure is unlikely to be enough to overcome your agoraphobia (a bit like having driving lessons but not putting in any practice!).

What is graded exposure?

The main CBT technique to overcome agoraphobia, graded exposure involves gradually facing your feared situations until anxiety subsides. As described in Section 2, avoiding or escaping from feared situations reduces the level of anxiety or panic you are feeling, but only for the short term.

Use the box provided to write down what you think would happen if you stayed in the situation that makes you anxious.

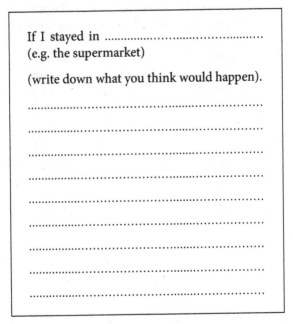

If I stayed in ....
(e.g. the supermarket)

(write down what you think would happen).

....

....

....

....

....

....

....

....

....

Would it surprise you to learn that by staying in the situation, your anxiety will naturally fall without having to do anything? Have a look at the following diagram that explains how this works. When we are afraid of a situation like going out, we will often try to avoid it. Avoidance is certainly effective at relieving anxiety but only at the time. Unfortunately, avoidance is a short-term solution that often leads to long-term difficulties because the vicious cycle of anxiety and avoidance is never broken. Graded exposure provides a useful way to break this vicious cycle by teaching you to slowly face the feared situation until anxiety falls.

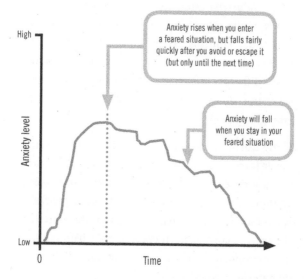

From Karina Lovell (1999)

By remaining in the situation, anxiety lessens. Continued avoidance means that a natural reduction in anxiety does not have an opportunity to happen, meaning that the level of perceived threat of going out stays the same.

It's likely that facing your agoraphobia head on using graded exposure sounds really hard, and it is hard but, believe me, it is possible. Try to think of a time in your life when you felt very anxious about something and, after practice, your anxiety was reduced. We could return to the example of learning to drive that was mentioned earlier in the book. To begin with, the learner driver might practise in an industrial estate in the evenings or on quiet roads, while others start with a driving instructor with dual controls. With repeated practice, the learner driver becomes more confident, tackling more difficult situations such as three-point turns, reversing round a corner, making a hill start and an emergency stop.

If the learner driver only read a book, they would never learn to drive, or if they practised for a minute at a time, it would take a long time to become confident, which is why driving lessons generally last for an hour. After regular and repeated practice, the driver's confidence increases. They begin to feel more comfortable on busy roads, at traffic lights and on entering and exiting roundabouts.

Use the next box to write down an example of when you have felt anxious, but after practising you have found it easier to do.

An example of when I have felt anxious about something, but after practising I found it easier to do.

....

....

....

....

....

....

There are four golden rules of exposure. The first is that it is 'graded', which means that you slowly begin to face your fears, starting with something that is easier and building up to harder situations (think of the learner driver starting on quiet roads). The second rule is that you need to practise the same situation 'repeatedly' (over and over again) until you feel less anxious (getting in lots of practice as you would have done while learning to drive). The third rule is you should stay in the feared situation ('prolonged') until your anxiety falls by at least 50 per cent (usually this takes between thirty and sixty minutes, but sometimes longer, so factor in ninety minutes if you can). The last principle is 'without distraction' so you are really focusing on what you are doing, rather than letting your mind take you elsewhere.

The Four Golden Rules of Exposure

- Graded – gradually facing your fears, starting with something easier and gently building up to more difficult situations.

- Repeated – exposure must be repeated; it is important that you practise facing your feared situations many times until you feel comfortable.

- Prolonged – stay in the situation long enough for your anxiety to fall by at least 50 per cent, which usually takes between thirty and sixty minutes but may take longer.

- Without distraction – distraction, which draws away our attention, reduces the experience and in so doing can interfere with the effectiveness of exposure. This means you should do your utmost to complete each exposure practice without any form of distraction.

Although exposure might sound daunting, I promise you, it's not impossible. It is useful to think of it in the following way: at present you are getting short-term relief by escaping and avoiding your fears, but this is not a long-term solution. Graded exposure will provoke short-term anxiety but lasting relief.

A warning regarding the use of controlled breathing and relaxation

A number of self-help texts suggest that people with agoraphobia should learn how to control their breathing and use relaxation strategies. It is not long ago that people would be advised to breathe into a paper bag to control their breathing; you might even have read something about that. It is true that over-breathing is likely to escalate symptoms and that steady even breathing is better, but trying to control breathing suggests that it is dangerous to over-breathe, and it isn't. Left alone, breathing will naturally go back to normal in time.

Likewise, being able to relax is obviously a good thing and it's important that we can all do it. However, learning to use relaxation as a strategy to stop symptoms of anxiety or panic suggests that these symptoms are dangerous so you should try to stop them. Actually, the reverse is true: it is better to let them happen as there is nothing dangerous about these symptoms.

The real danger here is that controlled breathing and relaxation can become two more safety behaviours that you definitely do not need. For this reason, no instruction is included here on how to control breathing or how to use relaxation strategies. You don't need it, so we won't do it.

Setting up your own individual exposure programme

You should have already determined your goals (pages 35–8); if not, it is important that you do this now. Once you have your goals, you're ready to set up your own exposure programme to help you to achieve these goals. Either on your own or with the help of a supporter, it is time to break these goals down into smaller steps and set some targets.

These targets need to be achievable, though they should also cause some anxiety. Remember that you need to make steady but gradual progress. So, start off slowly – don't overstretch as this can set you back a bit. A good way of doing this is to make a list of fears starting with the easiest; we'll do this shortly.

Key features of graded exposure

Graded exposure:

- Helps people to focus on the situations that trigger their fear.

- Provides a structured approach that enables a person to face their fears in a controlled way.

- Helps find a manageable starting point for the exposure by grading the feared situations from least to most feared.

- Enables the breaking of the vicious cycle of avoidance and leads to a decrease in anxiety.

- Allows feared situations to be conquered in a controlled way through using a 'ladder' of increasingly challenging situations.

- Allows you to reclaim your life as fear reduces or disappears.

Applying graded exposure involves going through four stages and we'll now go through each of them in turn.

Stages of graded exposure

- Stage 1: Identify feared situations.

- Stage 2: Grade these to create an exposure ladder.

- Stage 3: Set up conditions for graded exposure practice.

- Stage 4: Work your way up the ladder.

Stage 1: Identify feared situations

Feared situations are those that are avoided or, at times, experienced with extreme discomfort or distress and will be related to the goals you listed on pages 35–8.

Here are some questions that will help you to pinpoint your feared situations:

- In what way is your agoraphobia interfering with your life?

- What situations make you anxious?

- Are there any situations that you would like to stop avoiding?

- What have you stopped doing now that you used to do before your agoraphobia developed?

Zoe's feared situations

Going out alone

Being in a supermarket

Travelling by bus

Driving on the motorway

Going to the shopping centre

Travelling by train

Now take a moment to make a list of your feared situations.

My feared situations

....

....

....

....

....

....

....

....

Factors that can make the problem better or worse

Even though you may be fearful in a given situation, some factors may make it either easier or more difficult for you to tolerate. For example, supermarkets at busy times are likely to be more difficult than at quieter times. Going on public transport is probably easier when accompanied than when alone. Let's now try to think of all the different situations that are relevant to your agoraphobia. What would make it easier or more difficult for you? Here are some questions that should help you to pinpoint these moderating factors:

- What sort of things do you do that you find help to reduce your anxiety?

- Is there anything about the situation itself that makes it more or less intense for you?

- Does the time of day have any impact on your level of discomfort?

- What difference does it make if you're accompanied?

What affects Haider's level of anxiety that is associated with going to the cinema?

Having my walking stick relaxes me a bit.

Sitting near an exit at the end of a row helps.

I prefer matinées as it's generally quieter earlier in the day.

Being with my friend makes it possible.

What affects my level of anxiety that is associated with my feared situations?

....

....

....

....

....

....

....

....

You should now have a note of your feared situations and a list of things that affect the amount of anxiety you experience when in your feared situations.

Stage 2: Grade these to create an exposure ladder

The next step is to create an exposure 'ladder' out of the situations that you have described in the last two exercises. A ladder is a list of situations that involve exposing yourself to your anxiety-provoking situations, in order of increasing difficulty. The easiest is placed at the bottom rung of the ladder and the most difficult is at the top.

Think of it as tackling your agoraphobia like climbing a ladder; start on the first rung and find your footing before climbing to the next. For example, Zoe, who fears going out and travelling by public transport, had a list like this:

Zoe's anxiety stepladder

LEVEL OF ANXIETY	SITUATION CAUSING ANXIETY
Hardest	Go by train (alone)
	Go by train (accompanied)
	Drive on the motorway (alone)
	Drive on the motorway (accompanied)
	Go to shopping centre (alone)
	Go to shopping centre (accompanied)
	Go to the local town centre (alone)
	Go to the local town centre (accompanied)
	Go to the supermarket (alone)
	Go to the supermarket (accompanied)
	Go by bus (alone)
	Go by bus (accompanied)
	Go to the local shop (alone)
Easiest	Go to the local shop (accompanied)

Creating a ladder

- Combine the list of feared situations you made earlier with the situations that make them easier or more difficult, to produce a much longer list. The situations should always ultimately involve doing it alone, without a safety behaviour.

- Place them in order of difficulty, the easiest at the bottom and the hardest at the top.

- Only include situations on the stepladder that you can't do due to your agoraphobia. (There is a blank stepladder on page 164.)

In the following box, make your own list. If you find this difficult, use Zoe's example ladder as a guide or you might like to discuss it with your supporter if you have one. Now complete your ladder by placing each feared situation on a step of the ladder.

Feared situations and things
that affect my levels of anxiety

....

....

....

....

....

....

....

....

....

....

....

....

....

....

....

....

....

....

Well done! You have now completed most of the planning linked to getting started with graded exposure.

Stage 3: Set up conditions for graded exposure

Now we are going to use all of the hard work you've put into the last two stages to plan your first exposure practice. This practice will be planned in a way that will allow you to experience a reduction in your anxiety linked to the feared situation that you have placed on the lowest rung of your ladder. The idea is to plan how you are going to begin to face your fears in a way that you are in control and at a pace that is right for you. You may have tried to face your fears several times before. However, this time you will use the golden rules of exposure listed on pages 76–7. Can you remember what these are? If not, do go back to remind yourself before carrying on.

The first rung of the ladder should be challenging but not completely overwhelming. It is important that you can both succeed in your first exposure practice and experience a reduction of anxiety in the process. Quite often, people can imagine starting with an exposure practice that they predict will result in around 50/100 on their scale of anxiety. If you sense that this is too much for you to make a start, think about adding in a lower rung. You can have as many rungs as you like. Now let's plan an exposure practice that is based on this rung of the ladder.

Let's think of the practicalities involved in your first exposure practice. Here are some useful questions that Zoe considered before her first practice (which involved going to the local shop at a quiet time with her husband) that you can adapt for your own use:

- When am I going to do the first exposure practice? (Try to start your exposure practice as soon as possible. Putting it off can make getting started more difficult.)

- Who will come with me?

- How will this be arranged with them?

- What would be helpful to tell this person about my agoraphobia and will they be supportive (if not, you may want to choose another person)?

You will hopefully now have a date and a time for your first exposure practice. Remember that the exposure should be *prolonged*, so you should plan to allow at least an hour and ideally ninety minutes for this initially. You will need to stay in the situation until your level of anxiety *has reduced by at least*

50 per cent. So, if your level was 50/100 initially, stay in the situation until it is 25/100 (25 per cent) or lower. The length of your exposure practice is determined by the time it takes to achieve this 50 per cent reduction, *not by the duration alone*.

Another condition for graded exposure is that you should do it *without distraction*. This means that you should ideally not be doing things like playing on your phone, listening to music or chatting to someone. Being accompanied is a safety behaviour, so it is a good idea to factor this in on your ladder as having a supporter can really help when trying a new step, but ensure that you have a step where you do it alone too.

Some people find themselves needing to use some distraction techniques initially to help them cope with a situation. If this is the case for you, that's absolutely fine, but plan an additional rung on the ladder that involves an exposure practice where you do the same thing but without distraction. So, for instance, Zoe always has a step to try a new situation accompanied by her husband or friend which helps make her feel safer before the next step of doing it alone. That is absolutely fine, and a good thing to do.

Another principle linked to graded exposure is that it should be repeated. You will see that there is space on the record sheet for quite a few exposure practice sessions. You should try to undertake an exposure practice once a day for *at least* three days per week, but ideally every day. You might even carry out more than one a day. Haider started very slowly, but within a couple of weeks he was doing exposure practice in the morning and in the afternoon. The more often you do exposure, the quicker the progress you should make. If you are unable to practise exposure often enough, fear can creep back over the period in between which will place a limit on the speed you progress.

The success of graded exposure can be strengthened by introducing variation into the exposure practice. For example, Zoe went to a number of different supermarkets rather than the same one every time, and Haider went to three different cinemas.

Now you are ready to start your exposure! It is a good idea to complete some ratings of your anxiety over your exposure practice so you can see how it is going and know when your anxiety is low enough to leave. *Rate your level of anxiety every few minutes* and record the following on the 'Facing your agoraphobia record sheet':

1. Both the time and your level of anxiety at the start of the exposure practice.

2. Your level of anxiety at its highest point.

3. Both the time and your level of anxiety at the end of the practice (which should be at least 50 per cent less than it was when you started).

4. From the times recorded in 1) and 3), you can calculate the duration of the practice, which goes in the final column. This duration should help with the planning of future exposure practice.

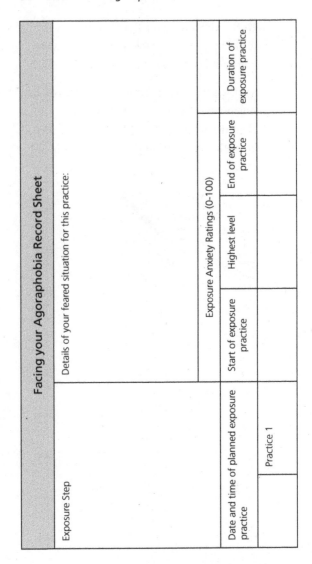

Facing your Agoraphobia Record Sheet

Exposure Step	Details of your feared situation for this practice:		
	Exposure Anxiety Ratings (0–100)		
	Start of exposure practice	Highest level	End of exposure practice	Duration of exposure practice
Date and time of planned exposure practice			
Practice 1			

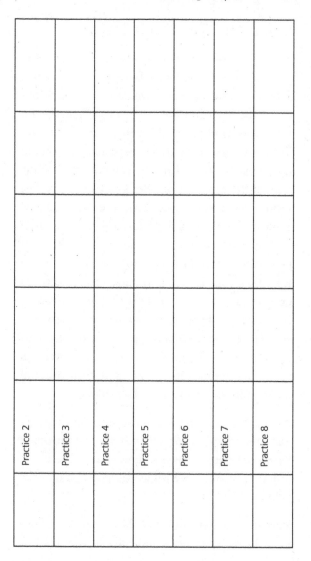

Practice 2	Practice 3	Practice 4	Practice 5	Practice 6	Practice 7	Practice 8

Stage 4: Climb the ladder

Begin exposure practice as soon as possible after you have constructed your ladder. Putting it off is a form of avoidance and it will feed into the vicious cycle. The first exposure will be to the situation on the first rung of your ladder. If you are able to follow the principles of graded exposure, you should notice that the level of anxiety you experience at the start of the exposure practice gradually decreases, session by session, over time. You are gradually allowing the fight-or-flight response to reset itself for this particular situation. How quickly this happens will vary from person to person. When you feel ready, you can begin to move up and start the exposure practice for the next rung of the ladder. As a rough guide, once your anxiety for a particular step has reduced to 20/100, providing that the steps on your ladder are fairly evenly spaced, there is a good chance that you will be more than ready to move up to the next rung of the ladder.

As you face agoraphobic situations, you may find that your level of anxiety differs from what you might have predicted. In such instances, feel free to re-order the steps as needed as you progress up your ladder.

Start a new worksheet for each step. There are more blank worksheets provided in the 'Further

Resources' section at the back of this book. If you carry out more than eight exposures for a particular step, you will need to start a second worksheet for that same step.

Key point

Remember to always follow the golden rules of exposure (pages 76–7) when planning and completing your exposure practice and continue to complete the worksheets. Most people say that this helps them, and you can look back over your worksheets to see the progress you have made. In turn, this should increase your confidence and encourage you to keep moving forward.

The process is repeated until you have achieved the goals that you listed on pages 35–8. You should be more able to meet these goals as your levels of anxiety decrease. When you are able to achieve all of the steps on your ladder, this is a natural place to end the exposure practice. This means that your agoraphobia is no longer significantly interfering with your life. Imagine how good that is going to feel!

See how Zoe worked through some of the steps on her ladder:

Week 1: Went to the local shops with my friend every day for at least one hour (four days) then alone for following three days.

Week 2: Went on a bus journey for at least an hour accompanied by my friend (four days) then alone for the following three days.

The idea is to carry on in this way until you have completed all the situations that make you anxious.

The role of a supporter

As mentioned earlier, many people find it helpful to have support from a relative or friend. Although a supporter is not necessary for doing graded exposure, they often help, particularly in the early stages when you are getting started. If you are working through the book with a healthcare professional, they will generally be happy to talk to your supporter together with you if you would like them to.

Troubleshooting

You might remember that I mentioned earlier that you are bound to encounter some stumbling blocks along the way. There are some common difficulties that people encounter when doing self-help for agoraphobia, so let's look at some of them now.

I don't know how to cope with the anxiety when facing my frightening situations

This is a common difficulty and there are a number of ways of coping with your anxiety. One way is to use coping statements. These are phrases that you can say to yourself or write down on a piece of card (often writing them down for the first few weeks is helpful and then try saying them to yourself). For example, they may include things like: 'Anxiety is unpleasant but it won't harm me'; 'Although I feel anxious now, I will feel better in the long run'; 'These feelings will pass'; 'I am not going to die'. These are just a few examples, and there are many more that you could come up with. It is important that they are relevant to you. In the box, write three coping statements that you think may be helpful for you. If this is hard to do, ask your supporter to help you, if you have one. Haider used this as one of his coping statements:

> These feelings will pass, just stay with it.
> You CAN do this!

Coping Statement 1

....

....

....

....

....

....

....

....

....

Coping Statement 2

....

....

....

....

....

....

....

....

....

> Coping Statement 3
>
> ....
> ....
> ....
> ....
> ....
> ....
> ....
> ....
> ....

I have managed to get so far but I just can't face the next step on my ladder

It is completely normal to get 'stuck' at some point while doing exposure. Often the reason for this is that the gap between the steps on the ladder is too big. This is a common problem and can be overcome by breaking the steps down into smaller ones. For example, Zoe managed her step of going on a bus while accompanied but found the next step on the list of going on a bus alone too difficult. There are a number of ways to break this down, for example:

- Your supporter being on the bus for only part of the journey.

- Asking someone to meet you at the bus stop.

- Having someone drive behind the bus.

These 'intermediate' steps eventually lead to you doing the original one without support.

I am much better now, and I want to stop taking my antidepressants – should I?

The answer to this question very much depends on how your mood has been. It is generally recommended that people who are depressed remain on antidepressants for at least six months after their depression has lifted. Please do not reduce your medication without discussing it with your doctor.

I have practised a step over and over again and the anxiety doesn't seem to be getting any better

There may be a number of reasons for this problem but the most common is that the person is continuing to avoid in some way. Such avoidance may not be obvious (for example, continuing to use a safety behaviour) and it may be that you are so used to doing it, you don't recognise it yourself! First, when you carry out your exposure, try to monitor yourself carefully (writing it down may help) to see if there are any 'hidden' avoidances. You could try looking at your list of safety behaviours from earlier in the book and see whether you are engaging in any. Sometimes people try to distract themselves by imagining that they are elsewhere. This is another safety behaviour and your anxiety is unlikely to improve on the step until you drop this; try to stay in the moment.

I have managed to stop the avoidance, but I still get the thoughts

This is a common problem and experience tells us that first the behaviour changes (i.e. going out, using public transport etc.) but people continue to have worrying thoughts (such as 'I might panic'). The good news is that these thoughts reduce in time as you get used to going out. It can just take a little while for your thoughts to catch up with your new behaviours.

What if I have a panic attack?

The idea of the ladder is to try to face your fears in a controlled way. Although it is crucial that you experience an increase in anxiety, panic attacks, while not at all dangerous, are horrible to experience so hopefully this will be rare or not happen at all. If you do have a panic attack, try to remember that symptoms are escalating because you are interpreting physical symptoms of anxiety in a catastrophic way. For example, the feeling of light-headedness could be interpreted as a sign of being about to collapse, increased heart rate as the start of a heart attack, breathlessness as suffocation, racing thoughts as going mad, and so on.

The initial trigger of the panic attack can be either 1) an internal one (e.g. a thought, image or bodily sensation – 'Ooh that was a nasty twinge there at the side of my head, that's not right, I'm having an aneurism'), or 2) an external one (e.g. a crowded shop) which is deemed to be threatening. Panic attacks start suddenly, are extremely distressing and last for several minutes, sometimes longer. However, I promise that they will pass without you having to do anything at all. If this happens to you, it might be that there is another step on the ladder that should be inserted between the last one and this one. Take a step back and work up to it again.

I was unable to finish the practice session, because I was too frightened

Sometimes people underestimate how much discomfort they will experience during an exposure practice and are unable to complete it. Don't worry if this happens to you. Here are some possible solutions:

- Adopt a coping strategy that will help you for this step, which can then be dropped in the future. One example of this is having someone with you during the exposure practice. Zoe adopted this approach for her ladder. Perhaps you could use a form of distraction to reduce the intensity of the experience and then drop this in a later exposure practice – Haider had his walking stick. Remember, these are safety behaviours, so ultimately you want to work up to doing the exposure without them.

- Construct an intermediate step on the ladder that is lower than the one you are attempting but still higher than the one that you have completed. That does not mean doing it for a shorter time though; the exposure practice should always be prolonged.

Although many of Haider's feared situations were similar to Zoe's, his ladder was a bit different from hers as he had chosen to try to overcome his agoraphobia alone at first. We can see how he incorporated steps that included using his walking stick at first before moving on to doing the step without the safety behaviour.

Haider's anxiety stepladder

LEVEL OF ANXIETY	SITUATION CAUSING ANXIETY
Hardest	Go to cinema and sit in middle of row
	Go to cinema and sit near exit
	Go on bus sitting at window near the back
	Go on bus and sit near the exit
	Go to the local town centre (alone)
	Go to the local town centre (accompanied)
	Go to local shopping precinct without stick
	Go to local shopping precinct with stick
	Go to the corner shop without stick
	Go to the corner shop with stick
	Go to the park without my stick
Easiest	Go to the park using my walking stick for balance

I stayed in the situation, but my anxiety didn't go down by 50 per cent

Here are some possible solutions to this problem:

- Increase the length of the exposure practice. Earlier it was suggested that you initially allow ninety minutes for exposure, but for some people it can take longer.

- Once again, you can construct a step on the ladder that is lower than the one you are attempting but still higher than the one that you have completed.

- Check that you are not taking any medication or using any other substances (such as caffeine) that might be interfering with the process. If relevant, it might be useful to discuss this topic with your doctor.

Incidentally, the reason why it is advised that some medications for psychological problems (or other substances such as alcohol) are not used at the same time as graded exposure is that they can also interfere with this process. Consequently, when you reduce the dose, the level of anxiety can rise again.

My anxiety reduced within the exposure practice but does not go down between each practice, so my peak anxiety remains quite similar each time

Sometimes people who are also experiencing depression can find this to be an issue. If this is the case for you, seek treatment for your depression first and then come back to graded exposure later when your mood has improved.

I want to do the exposure, but other things are getting in the way

Perhaps the time is not right for you at the moment to start exposure for your agoraphobia. Do you think this might be the case? If so, don't worry. Come back to it when you have more space in your life; it is vital that you can dedicate time to overcoming your agoraphobia, so do it when it is right for you. Beware of putting things off because you are scared, though; that is a different issue altogether.

You might be feeling a bit overwhelmed at the idea of facing some challenging situations and reading about some of the issues that can arise. Don't worry! By the time you will be considering the more challenging steps on your ladder, they will seem less difficult. The fifth rung of the ladder can seem impossible when you are about to start on your first rung, but by the time you have achieved the fourth rung, moving up to the fifth is no bigger a step than the last.

This has been an important section for getting you going with your exposure. Carry on working up your ladder until you reach the top. You can do it!

THE RELAPSE MANAGEMENT TOOLKIT

Hopefully, by now you have a better understanding of some of the factors that have been keeping your agoraphobia going, and have made some changes to how you deal with these difficult situations. Most of all, I hope that you are feeling better and that you are able to do more and enjoy life outside your home.

If you have carefully worked your way through this book and agoraphobia is still interfering with your life, it might be an idea to seek help from your doctor or other healthcare professional.

If you have made improvements, that's fantastic. I hope that you are now making progress towards meeting the goals that you made at the start of this journey (we'll revisit these later). Please continue to use exposure and you should find that entering these difficult situations becomes increasingly like second nature.

CBT self-help books like this have helped lots of people overcome their problems, and the majority of those people stay well. However, as mentioned in Section 2, it is also natural that you may experience the occasional setback on your road to recovery, a time when you might find it harder to go out and do the things that you want to do.

Through your own hard work, you have successfully helped yourself to feel better. Now we need to keep an eye on this and check that you don't slip back into the vicious cycle of avoidance again. This is the final stage – staying well and dealing with any difficulties that you may encounter in the future. To increase the chances of you staying well and keeping in your positive cycle, please work through this section. You've worked hard and now it's important to maintain what you have gained.

You may worry that you will lose some of the progress that you've made or worry about your agoraphobia coming back again in the future (this is called a 'relapse'). You might have some questions such as:

'Will I cope by myself?'

'What do I do if I start avoiding again?'

'Is there still work that I need to do to keep on top of my agoraphobia?'

'Will I slip back into my old habits?'

Once you begin to feel better, understandably you will want to maintain the positive changes that you've achieved. It can be frightening to think that you might slip back and your life become limited by fear again.

If a healthcare professional has supported your efforts through the use of this book, being discharged from their care may also produce concerns for you about whether you can now cope alone. A key thing to remember is that it wasn't the support from the professional that resulted in your progress. Rather, it was the result of the hard work that *you* put into the exposure practice. It was *your* application of the knowledge and techniques that *you* have learned in this book that produced your recovery. You can successfully apply these techniques in the future if you need to. The use of this toolkit will help you to keep on track.

Setbacks

Life is full of ups and downs. Depending on how you are feeling, even something small can trigger a setback. Stressful situations can often cause problems, for example if you argue with a good friend; you or a loved one becomes ill; your children are sitting exams; you apply for a job and don't get it; your finances are stretched. The list is endless.

What is important is identifying the situations that might lead to a setback and planning how you can deal with these situations before they cause problems. Some setbacks can't be anticipated and planned for, so it is important to know the warning signs so that you can identify when it might be about to begin and then put in place a plan for how to cope in order that the setback is short-lived and as mild as possible. In Section 5, you will read about Zoe's and Haider's setbacks and how they dealt with them.

Take a moment to think about what sorts of situations have contributed to making your agoraphobia worse over the years. Write them down in the box provided.

> **Situations that have contributed to making my agoraphobia worse:**
>
> ....
>
> ....
>
> ....
>
> ....
>
> ....
>
> ....
>
> ....
>
> ....

Now spend some time thinking about the situations you identified that made your agoraphobia worse. In particular, try to remember how you reacted to these situations in terms of your feelings, physical symptoms, thoughts and behaviours. Next, think of as many situations as you can that might lead to a setback for you in the coming months and years. Make a note of these in the box provided.

Situations that might lead to a setback in the coming months and years:

....

....

....

....

....

....

....

....

At stressful times, you may begin to again avoid situations that were related to your agoraphobia. This is termed a 'lapse' – a temporary return of symptoms. You may then worry that you are going to 'relapse' and your problem will return.

What's the difference between a lapse and a relapse?

A *lapse* is a brief return to feeling more fearful or avoiding situations again in a way that might interfere with your life. Lapses are normal and occur occasionally. So long as you put into practice the principles of graded exposure, you can quickly get back on track again.

A lapse can become a *relapse*, when fear and avoidance return over a longer period, if it is allowed to 'take hold'. The vicious cycle gets going and the agoraphobia begins to significantly interfere with your lifestyle once again. The difference this time is that you now have the knowledge and skills to reapply the techniques you have learned and recover. You know the principles of exposure and how it works.

You may begin to feel hopeless about things, which will worsen matters. Try to be patient and compassionate with yourself. See a lapse for what it is: just a temporary 'blip'. Try not to let it undermine your confidence by thinking of the worst-case scenario. If you do think negatively in this way, it may mean that you switch into the vicious cycle of avoidance again. Try not to avoid. The task of recovery is easier if you catch it quickly before old habits become engrained into your lifestyle again. This is the reason why it is helpful to learn to notice the early warning signs (or 'red flags') that indicate that things may be slipping backwards.

If at all possible, try to keep doing all of the things that you have managed to achieve on your ladder. If some of the rungs have become a bit more difficult, get going with the exposure practice again to build up your confidence. This will help prevent a lapse from becoming a relapse. Don't give up. You know what works for you. Reapply the exposure techniques and they will help you again.

Important: Setbacks may occur. Be realistic: you are likely to experience them at times. Recognise them for what they are and not as a sign that you have gone back to square one.

You have the tools to prevent a lapse from becoming a relapse. You know the function of the symptoms. You know how to overcome your agoraphobia if it persists. Don't imagine a 'doomsday' scenario where all your problems are flooding back. You will tend to remain in your positive cycle by:

- Keeping things in proportion and remembering that you have the tools to overcome any issues if need be.

- Maintaining a pattern of behaviour where you are generally approaching situations relating to your agoraphobia rather than starting to avoid them again.

Try going back through Section 3 and reapplying the techniques. This may increase your confidence and help you to get on top of your fears before things build up and possibly develop into agoraphobia again.

Hopefully, you will have learned from using this self-help book that techniques are available to help you to help yourself. Also, these can continue to be put into action in the future if you feel the need to do so. Making a relapse management plan and carrying it out when needed reduces the likelihood that you will slip back and that your agoraphobia will return. It will also ensure that you have the confidence to spot any early warning signs or 'red flags'. This insight will allow you to get on top of any symptoms as they occur.

You can think of this section as a toolkit to help you:

- Recognise red flag situations that might lead you to start avoiding again.

- Challenge a belief that a return of some anxiety must indicate that your agoraphobia has returned.

- Put into place strategies to prevent a lapse becoming a relapse.

- Know where to get help and support in the future should you need it.

My early warning signs

The first step in thinking about the future and dealing with any setbacks is to mentally make a note of the things you might notice if your agoraphobia begins to take hold. You may want to put this to the back of your mind but please do try to spend some time thinking about it. These are the things that may indicate that problems are starting to come back. If you notice the signs and take early action, this can allow you to get on top of them before they begin to take hold and have an impact on your life.

In the next diagram, write down the things you think you are likely to experience as the first sign of problems recurring. Think back to a time when your agoraphobia was first developing. Write down the changes that you noticed in the following areas:

- Your *feelings*

- Patterns in your *thinking*

- The *physical feelings* in your *body*

- Your *behaviours*; what you did more or less of (make sure you think about escape, avoidance and safety behaviours)

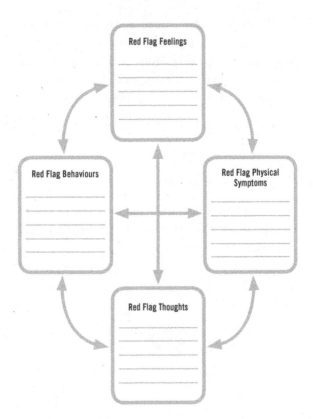

Red flags that you noticed when you first experienced agoraphobia

To help you complete this diagram, it might be a good idea to turn back to the similar one you completed on page 41. Think back to the time when you first noticed your agoraphobia.

If you have had agoraphobia for a long time, it might be hard to remember how it started. You could speak to someone who knew you well over this period of time when your agoraphobia was developing. Often, other people can start to see change before we notice it ourselves. They can have some helpful observations. Perhaps they noticed that you were starting to avoid going to some places by yourself. It might be that you were doing more negative things to help you to cope (for instance, using alcohol to help you to go out). It may be that you started to need help for some things that you used to do on your own. They might remember you saying that you couldn't do some things or making excuses not to go places (for example, saying that you preferred to buy online rather than go shopping with a friend). Perhaps they noticed that you were experiencing some physical symptoms in certain situations. It might be that you began to say that you were experiencing anxiety. Maybe they noticed that you wouldn't go anywhere without something that made you feel safe (remember Haider with his walking stick). Perhaps you became more tense or irritable more generally.

My red flags

My early warning signs are:

....

....

....

....

....

....

....

....

....

....

....

....

....

....

If you feel comfortable to do so, share your relapse management plan with someone you trust and see regularly. If you or that person notices that red flags are creeping back into your life, it is a good indicator that you need to take action. Use graded exposure in the same way that you did before. If you catch it early, it should be reasonably straightforward to regain the progress you'd made previously.

Haider's mum noticed that he had started to avoid going to the supermarket on the bus and was ordering shopping online again. After his mum pointed this out, he realised that he was slipping back into an avoidance cycle. Haider went back to his ladder and started working on bus travel and going to the supermarket again until his anxiety level came back down. He cancelled his supermarket online account and made a point of going grocery shopping to the supermarket by bus twice a week to rebuild his confidence.

How things have improved since you started reading this book

Reflecting on what you have achieved is an important part of relapse management. In the box below, list some of the improvements that you have noticed since you started working on your agoraphobia.

These might be linked to your symptoms (feelings, physical symptoms, thoughts and behaviours) and, importantly, also your lifestyle. Aspects of your lifestyle that might have changed include your:

- Relationships and social life (with partner, family, work colleagues and friends).

- Work life or ability to do other meaningful activities, such as voluntary work or being a carer for others.

- Ability to do essential things outside the house like going to the bank, filling the car with petrol, shopping.

- Hobbies (solo ones such as going to the gym, as well as group activities such as team sports or dancing).

In the boxes below, identify any positive improvements in these areas:

Symptoms

Relationships and social life

Work or other meaningful activity

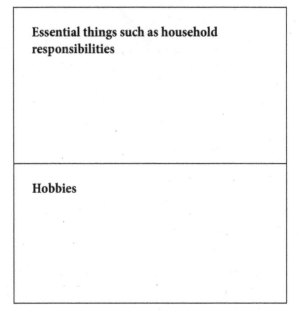

Essential things such as household responsibilities

Hobbies

Re-rating your goals

In Section 1, you set some goals for yourself. You can now re-rate them either by returning to the form that you used in Section 1 or by using the worksheet here. If possible, try to rate the goals without looking at your previous ratings. Once you have rated them, review the progress you have made by comparing each of them with your first ratings to see how they have changed. Sometimes, when change happens steadily, week by week, it is easy to lose track of all the progress you have made since the start, so this should help you to get a good sense of how much progress you have made.

My goals for feeling better

Goal 1: ....

....

....Today's date___/___/___

I can do this now (end of treatment rating; circle a number):

0	1	2	3	4	5	6
Not at all		Occasionally		Often		Any time

Goal 2: ....

....

.............................Today's date___/___/___

I can do this now (end of treatment rating; circle a number):

0	1	2	3	4	5	6
Not at all		Occasionally		Often		Any time

Goal 3: ....

....

.............................Today's date___/___/___

I can do this now (end of treatment rating; circle a number):

0	1	2	3	4	5	6
Not at all		Occasionally		Often		Any time

Take a moment to reflect on how far you have come. Perhaps there are other things that have changed that

I have not asked you about. Perhaps you feel *happier* now that you have got on top of your agoraphobia.

What helped things to improve?

What was it you did that helped you get on top of your agoraphobia? If you were to able to go back in time and offer yourself some advice when you were just starting to work on your agoraphobia, what advice would that be? For example, perhaps you might instruct yourself to be patient within the exposure practice or to make sure that you allow sufficient time? Perhaps you might say that it is important to generally approach rather than avoid? Make a note of this advice.

General advice

....

....

....

....

....

Now think about what advice you might give yourself if you became aware of a red flag situation that could lead to a lapse. Perhaps the advice would be quite similar to what you have just noted, or it might be completely different. For example, you might say that it is important to review your ratings on your 'ladder' once again and reinstate exposure practice as soon as you become aware of the lapse.

Advice in case of a red flag or lapse

....

....

....

....

....

The wellbeing review

The other really helpful strategy that you are likely to find useful is scheduling regular wellbeing reviews.

Ideally, mark a day in your calendar each month to prompt you to undertake a wellbeing review. Having a review day will help you to spot red flags sooner and ensure that you put into practice what you have learned in the book. Here is a structure to think through during your wellbeing review. It should take around twenty to thirty minutes and is an opportunity to stop, think and reflect on how you are doing and make any necessary changes at an early stage if needed.

My wellbeing review

Review date:

What have my symptoms been like over the past month?

Reading through my red flags list, have I had any experiences that have concerned me?

Do I need to take any action now to keep on top of my agoraphobia?

If so, what will be helpful to use in my toolkit?

What do I need to do and when am I going to do it?

The date of my next review is:

Is there anything else that you would like to work on?

Sometimes there are other areas in life in which people would like to see change. These might be goals you set at the start of the book that you would like to work on further or perhaps new things that you would now like to do. Some of your goals may not be completely met yet. Are there any difficulties that are getting in the way if this is the case? It is worth noting these down so you can remember them for later.

For the moment, it is probably best that you simply focus on maintaining the progress you have made so far. Once you have found that you have maintained progress for a few months, that is a good time to return to this list. Depending on what problems remain, it may be that you can either apply graded exposure to allow you to make progress or use another book from the *How to Beat* series. The other books are structured very similarly to this one but focus on other problems. If you have managed to use this book, you should cope very well with the others in the series should you need them.

If you are being supported by a healthcare professional, they should be able to help you decide how to move forward.

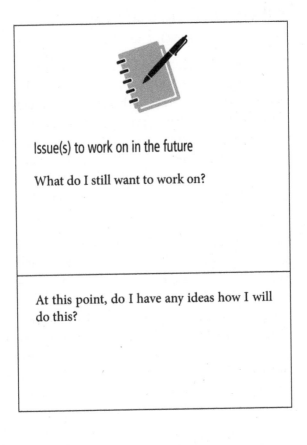

Issue(s) to work on in the future

What do I still want to work on?

At this point, do I have any ideas how I will do this?

When do I plan to do it (perhaps add in a reminder on my calendar for six months' time)?

Are there any resources that I need to get hold of to help with this?

Are there any things that might get in the way of me working on this, and how might I overcome these?

Relapse management top tips

Here are some top tips that may help you to use your toolkit to stay well:

1. The best way to prevent a lapse is to keep applying your exposure skills to maintain confidence. Remember the driving example? Just because you have passed your test doesn't mean you won't keep learning and building your confidence over time. Perhaps, every so often, try to do new things that create a little anxiety. Use the principles of exposure to get on top of this anxiety if you need to. Maybe you could learn a new hobby that takes you out of the home and lasts at least an hour.

2. Know your red flags. Watch out for times when you feel more stressed or when there is a lot of change in your life. If you have shared your red flags with others, they may be able to notice early negative changes in your symptoms.

3. Complete a wellbeing review even if you have been feeling well. It will remind you to keep going with what has been successful.

4. Check that you haven't crept back into an avoidance cycle in any aspect of your life. If so, think about how you can apply exposure to get back to approaching situations again.

5. Try not to be self-critical. Everyone is likely to experience setbacks at times. These are the body's natural response to situations that feel threatening. Focus on what you need to do to stop a lapse from becoming a relapse.

6. The thought of having to focus on using exposure again can feel a little disheartening. Try to focus on how effective it was for you before in addressing your agoraphobia. If it worked for you before, it is very likely to work again.

7. Use your toolkit as often as you need to and remember to carry out your wellbeing reviews. These don't have to be monthly. You may want to make them more frequent at first or if you have a setback. When you feel more confident in maintaining your progress, you can space the reviews out again.

Getting further help if you need it

Sometimes, despite your best efforts, you may still feel that you require additional help. Knowing where and how to get help is an important final component of your toolkit. There are some organisations that may be able to support you listed in the 'Further resources' at the back of the book, alongside spare copies of record sheets that you will need for continued practice. Now is a good time to think about some of the people around you who can form part of your 'wellbeing team'.

Think of people around you who you trust and who can support you. Could you share your toolkit with them so they can help you to watch out for red flags? Having read your toolkit, they will be aware of what you might need in order to feel better. Perhaps they can prompt you to access that? Write down the name of anyone you think would be a good supporter in that role.

....

....

....

....

....

Your doctor will usually be a key figure in your support plan. You may have been seeing your doctor periodically while you've been working through this book. If you need support, remember that they are there to offer medical advice and they should also be able to refer you, as needed, to expert healthcare professionals.

My doctor's name

....

....

My doctor's telephone number

....

....

Finally, make a note of any organisations from the 'Further resources' that you may want to contact should you need any further support. You can contact them when you are well and at your best, just so that you are sure that they are the right people to contact if you are experiencing difficulties.

....

....

....

....

....

Congratulations!

You've come a long way to reach this point and I'm delighted that you have managed to complete the exposure and stay with the book. Take a moment to think about the progress that you've made towards your goals. The journey may not have been easy. The progress you have made is down to you! This book has just provided you with some tools to allow you to help yourself. Be proud of what you have achieved. Perhaps you can apply some of these principles to other areas of your life to help you to achieve other goals. In life, generally speaking, approaching is a much better strategy than avoidance for solving problems.

This relapse management section will help you to keep hold of this progress. It will alert you when to put the necessary tools back into action if that situation arises. This book will always be here if you need it again.

In the next section, we return to Zoe and Haider's stories. They will relate how they used CBT self-help to get on top of their agoraphobia. Some people write down their own story in the way that Zoe and Haider have told theirs. It acts as a reminder of what they have achieved. Others might write a shorter letter to themselves to celebrate their progress. Perhaps you could write your story in this kind of way after reading their recovery stories. You could write this as if it were a letter to yourself in the future, rather like a paper time capsule. Pieces of writing like this can also be added to the toolkit if you wish. You can then re-read them as part of your wellbeing reviews, adding to them every so often as needed.

Remember the 'Further resources' section, which has some blank record sheets and details of some organisations that may be of help.

You should now have all the tools you need to keep your agoraphobia in check in the future. I wish you well.

RECOVERY STORIES

Zoe's story

Zoe is mum to a four-year-old son and was introduced on page 42. She'd had agoraphobia for around ten years and used graded exposure to tackle her problem. Here is Zoe's recovery story. Remember that more details of her agoraphobia and 'ladder' are on pages 42–4 and 86.

" My agoraphobia started with a panic attack when I was on a bus one day. It just seemed to come out of the blue and was so horrible I thought I was going to collapse. My heart was pounding, I was hot and sweaty, and my stomach was doing somersaults. I ended up feeling like everything was closing in on me. I actually thought I was going to die! I didn't understand what was happening to me. I got a terrible fright. I didn't get on a bus again for a few days, then I tried to catch a bus into town, but I started to feel anxious, so I came home. I couldn't face going through that again. I actually tried to get on a bus a few more times after that but I just never managed it, I always came home. It was extremely limiting as I was really quite reliant on the bus to get around. I then learned to drive, which helped a lot. I got my freedom back, but I never liked motorways. I would get the same symptoms that I experienced on the bus, so I avoided motorways too. It would take me ages getting to my parents' house as I had to take back roads instead of the motorway, adding a good half hour to my journey.

It carried on like that for years, I just adapted. Then around six years later, Zachary was born. I don't know why but I seemed to get worse from then on. I was generally just a bit more anxious. Zachary would have been about six months old when I had a panic attack when we were in the car driving to a friend's house for lunch. It was the same symptoms again. It was terrifying as I was worried I was going to lose control of the car and that I would kill us both. Anyway, I managed to pull over and I had to call my husband, who came and picked us up and took us home. I was in a terrible state. It was a hassle trying to get the car back, but a friend of my husband's helped to do it. After that I avoided driving altogether; it just seemed too risky especially as I would usually have Zachary in the car.

It was soon after that I began to feel anxious in shops. I was with my mum at a big out-of-town shopping centre and I started feeling panicky and I thought I was going to collapse. I came straight home. The same thing happened in a supermarket soon after when I was on my own and I just left a full basket and dashed home. My life was now getting really restricted, but I found ways round it. I became completely reliant on my husband and a close friend to take me places and to stay with me in case anything bad happened. I felt safe with them. But it was no way to live, I was completely dependent on others and that's not me.

I carried on like that for quite a long time. It got to a stage when I was worried that I would end up not being able to leave the house at all. I also started worrying that I wouldn't be able to take Zachary to school. It was really getting me down. I ended up quite depressed and my doctor prescribed me antidepressants. I'm not sure that they made me less agoraphobic, but they certainly helped my mood so that I had the get-up-and-go to do something about it. At that stage, I didn't even really know what agoraphobia was. I was seeing the doctor to review how the medication was going and I told her more about the problem and said I would like some help. She was able to tell me all about agoraphobia; it was like she was describing me to a tee. She was great actually, really empathic. Anyway, she suggested I might like to try self-help and encouraged me to bring my husband and friend on board to help me. I was a bit sceptical at first, like, how can I overcome a ten-year problem by myself with a book?!

Anyway, I agreed to give it a go. I had nothing to lose and so much to gain. The last thing I wanted was for my agoraphobia to impact on my son's life, so that really spurred me on.

So, I started reading up about agoraphobia and could see that I was almost a 'classic case'! That was reassuring in some ways, as sometimes I felt so alone with it. It also helped explain why the problem had got worse over the years as it crept into various areas of my life. I took a good hard look at what I had given up over the years and set those as my goals. In for a penny, in for a pound; I might as well aim for what I used to be able to do and reclaim my life.

My husband and friend were super-keen to help me, which was great as I think I would have struggled to do it myself. They even helped me create a ladder to work towards my goals. It was fairly straightforward in theory: do each step with someone first and then do it alone. It wasn't quite like that though!

So, exposure! Well it all makes sense, but just the thought of it was scary at first – let alone doing it. Anyway, my friend and husband were so encouraging, which was what I needed as I nearly ditched the idea a few times before I even started. I set a date then got cracking. I went to a local shop first with my husband. It was only a couple of streets away and is a mini supermarket. It was OK really. My anxiety went up at first but levelled off quicker than I thought, then started to come down. I did that a few times and started separating off from my husband so he would be in a different aisle from me and then, after a few times, just waiting at the door. I was so chuffed with myself. Next, he started waiting in the car for me, then when it came to going by myself, he picked me up a few times, which made me feel a bit more reassured that if anything went wrong, he would soon be there. That was a safety behaviour of course, so once I got more confident being in there by myself, we knocked that on the head and I started walking there and back too. What a boost that was.

I'd love to say that it was all plain sailing, but it wasn't. When I got to the step on the ladder of tackling buses, I really struggled moving from 'accompanied' to 'alone'. It was like I hit a wall with it and got completely stuck. Then we put in a few extra steps that involved my friend and my husband coming together on this one. I set off with my husband and he got off three stops before I did. My friend picked him up and they both met me when I got off at the other end. Then I got the bus back on my own and they met me at the bus stop near the house. Going homeward bound is easier than heading away from home, I discovered. Anyway, that all did the trick, and soon I was able to do it by myself. It felt fantastic conquering the bus avoidance and gave me so much more freedom.

I carried on like that just working away at the ladder until I got to the top. What a wonderful feeling that was. My friend and husband helped me with my relapse management plan and we were able to think of what my red flags are. So far so good! It has been four months now since I got to the top of my ladder. I talked to my doctor about coming off my antidepressants and she is happy for me to do that but wants me to wait until I've been feeling like this for at least six months, which will be in just a few more weeks, and then we will look at me reducing and coming off the medication. I have my life back and it feels great!"

Haider's story

Haider is a man in his fifties who lives alone and was introduced on page 44. He'd had agoraphobia for nearly thirty years and used graded exposure to tackle his problem. Here is Haider's recovery story. Remember that more details of his agoraphobia and goals are on pages 44–6.

" I'd had agoraphobia for a long time before I felt like I really had to do something about it. Previously I'd had a long illness that meant I was indoors for a long time, and then when it eventually came to going out again, I just felt like I couldn't. It seemed really odd to me that I started getting all these symptoms of anxiety when I went to go out for the first time. My heart was racing, I had a tight chest and felt lightheaded. I was worried that I might get ill and have a heart attack. It wasn't like my illness had anything to do with my heart but that was how it felt. It started like that and I stopped even trying to go out. It's pretty easy to just buy everything online and my mum would come round and drop other stuff off that I needed. It was no life though.

My good friend would take me to the cinema every couple of weeks or so in his car. We'd have to sit near the exit and at the end of a row so I could get out quickly if I started to feel unwell. I generally had a walking stick with me, not that I needed or used it; rather it was in case I felt lightheaded, I would have something to lean on to keep my balance.

My fifty-fifth birthday was approaching, and I just got to thinking, 'Is this what the rest of my life is going to look like?' I really didn't want that to be the case. I missed the freedom to go 'where I wanted, when I wanted' and was keen to find some other work that would get me out the house. I didn't say anything to anyone, but I started researching agoraphobia and reading up about the best ways to tackle it. I tried some alternative remedies first, but they didn't help. Graded exposure was something that kept coming up in my online searches. So that's what I decided to do.

I gave a lot of thought to what I wanted to get out of life, and I ended up with a really long list. I managed to whittle it down though, to be able to go shopping and travelling on public transport on my own and, as film has always been my passion, going to the cinema. All the other stuff would be doable if I conquered those things. The stuff I read suggested getting someone to support me, but I really wanted to do it alone. I wanted to surprise my mum and friend, to show them that I could do it.

Anyway, I put together a ladder of things to do and started with a reasonably easy step of just going out in the front garden and into the street. I decided to send a card to my mum as there is a post box at the end of my street. I managed it, but when I got back to the house, I felt worse than when I left. I forced myself to do it a few times that week, but it didn't feel any easier. It wasn't until I re-read the principles of exposure that I realised that I wasn't doing it in a prolonged way, rather I was doing it in short bursts. I've got a park opposite my house, and the next day it was sunny and fairly warm so I decided I would go to the park and walk around for a while and see how I got on. I took my walking stick with me just in case but did my best not to use it. I learned that the stick was a safety behaviour, so I inserted a step that meant doing stuff at first with the stick and then without. By the end of the week, the park visits were relatively easy, and I was ready to move on.

I worked my way up the ladder on my own but got to the stage where I felt that I could do with some help. So I asked my friend when we went to the cinema if we could sit a bit further from the exit and I would sit a couple of seats in. That worked well and eventually we moved up to us going together, but I went in one theatre to watch a film by myself and he went in another and we met at the end. That was liberating.

Unfortunately, my mum died soon after I finally got on top of going to the supermarket. She'd spotted the signs when I had started to avoid doing it and had really helped me get back on track. Her death really set me back. I felt so low and really couldn't be bothered battling to overcome my agoraphobia or even to stay on top of where I had got to. I just gave up. I phoned the Samaritans a couple of times, just for someone to talk to about my grief and how I was feeling. That helped a lot. It took me a couple of months to restart and although I had to begin close to the bottom of the ladder again, I did find that I got to the next steps quicker this time around.

I had a few more hiccups along the way but nothing as bad as losing my mum. It probably took me close to six months to get on top of it. Not being restricted like I was has given me a new lease of life and I know my mum would be proud. I have even joined a local gym, which gets me out and it's also getting me fit. I am planning a holiday abroad, something that was inconceivable only a few months ago. I've even been to a film festival by train and stayed overnight. I've not had much luck on the job front so far but I'm about to start a night class (another big thing!) and hope to learn a new skill that might help me in my job hunting.

If I could give one piece of advice to someone else with agoraphobia, I would tell them to do their utmost to reclaim their life. It is not necessarily easy but when you accomplish a step, it is so fantastic, and when you get to the top of your ladder you'll feel like shouting it from the rooftops, so don't give up. Although I was keen to sort it out by myself, I would also suggest that it's worth having someone to help with some of the steps if you can.

My red flags

My early warning signs are:

Stopping going to the gym

Only being able to go to the cinema
with a friend

Not going to the shops

Avoiding bus travel

My wellbeing review

Review date:

3rd March

What have my symptoms been like over the
past month?

Pretty good. I've had the odd time
when I have felt a bit jittery but I'm
not avoiding doing anything.

Reading through my red flags list, have I had any experiences that have concerned me?

Not really. I did have an urge to just get all my shopping online last week, but I reminded myself that I shouldn't just stay in because it's raining. What if it rains for a month, where will I be? So, I went, and it was fine. I know I need to push myself when the weather is bad or I can't be bothered, but I think that's normal, well it is for me anyway.

Do I need to take any action now to keep on top of my fear?

Not this month. I'm doing stuff, going to the gym etc., and enjoying it. Nice to feel fit again!

If so, what will be helpful to use in my toolkit?

Not necessary this month, I just need to continue the way I am, but I check my red flags once every couple of weeks to make sure.

What do I need to do and when am I going to do it?

N/A

The date of my next review is:

3rd April."

FURTHER RESOURCES

My goals for feeling better

Goal 1: ....

....

....

I can do this now   (Today's date___/___/___)
(circle a number):

  0   1   2   3   4   5   6

Not at all   Occasionally   Often   Any time

One-month re-rating   (date___/___/___)
(circle a number):

  0   1   2   3   4   5   6

Not at all   Occasionally   Often   Any time

Two-month re-rating   (date___/___/___)
(circle a number):

  0   1   2   3   4   5   6

Not at all   Occasionally   Often   Any time

Three-month re-rating   (date__/__/__)
(circle a number):

   0   1   2   3   4   5   6

Not at all   Occasionally   Often   Any time

Goal 2: ....

....

....

I can do this now   (Today's date__/__/__)
(circle a number):

   0   1   2   3   4   5   6

Not at all   Occasionally   Often   Any time

One-month re-rating   (date__/__/__)
(circle a number):

   0   1   2   3   4   5   6

Not at all   Occasionally   Often   Any time

Two-month re-rating   (date__/__/__)
(circle a number):

   0   1   2   3   4   5   6

Not at all   Occasionally   Often   Any time

Three-month re-rating   (date___/___/___)
(circle a number):

   0   1   2   3   4   5   6
  Not at all   Occasionally   Often   Any time

Goal 3: ....

....

....

I can do this now   (Today's date___/___/___)
(circle a number):

   0   1   2   3   4   5   6
  Not at all   Occasionally   Often   Any time

One-month re-rating   (date___/___/___)
(circle a number):

   0   1   2   3   4   5   6
  Not at all   Occasionally   Often   Any time

Two-month re-rating   (date___/___/___)
(circle a number):

   0   1   2   3   4   5   6
  Not at all   Occasionally   Often   Any time

Three-month re-rating   (date___/___/___)
(circle a number):

  0   1   2   3   4   5   6
 Not at all   Occasionally   Often   Any time

My stepladder

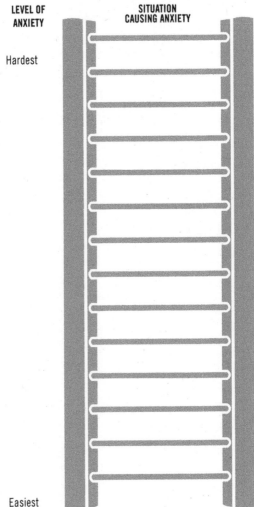

My stepladder

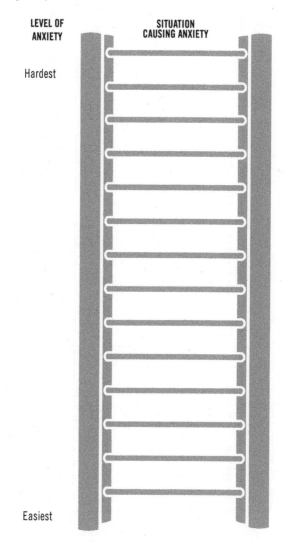

Facing your Agoraphobia Record Sheet

Exposure Step	Details of your feared situation for this practice:		
Date and time of planned exposure practice	Exposure Anxiety Ratings (0-100)		
	Start of exposure practice	Highest level	End of exposure practice	Duration of exposure practice
Practice 1				

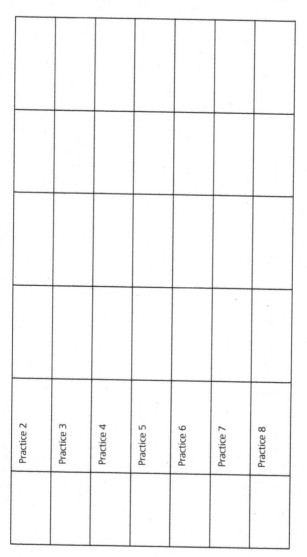

	Practice 2	Practice 3	Practice 4	Practice 5	Practice 6	Practice 7	Practice 8

Facing your Agoraphobia Record Sheet

Exposure Step	Details of your feared situation for this practice:			
		Exposure Anxiety Ratings (0–100)		
Date and time of planned exposure practice		Start of exposure practice	Highest level	End of exposure practice	Duration of exposure practice
	Practice 1				

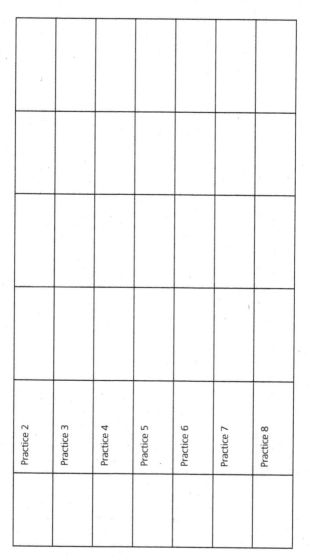

Practice 2				
Practice 3				
Practice 4				
Practice 5				
Practice 6				
Practice 7				
Practice 8				

Facing your Agoraphobia Record Sheet

Exposure Step	Details of your feared situation for this practice:			
		Exposure Anxiety Ratings (0-100)		
Date and time of planned exposure practice		Start of exposure practice	Highest level	End of exposure practice	Duration of exposure practice
	Practice 1				

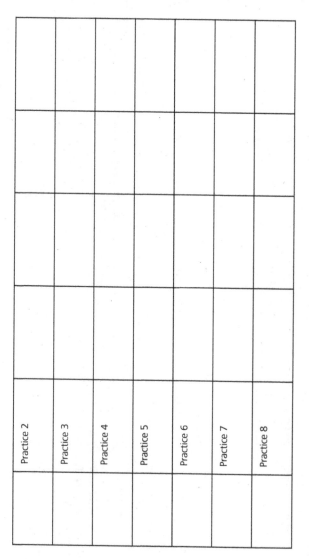

					Practice 2	
					Practice 3	
					Practice 4	
					Practice 5	
					Practice 6	
					Practice 7	
					Practice 8	

Facing your Agoraphobia Record Sheet

Exposure Step

Details of your feared situation for this practice:

Date and time of planned exposure practice		Exposure Anxiety Ratings (0–100)			
		Start of exposure practice	Highest level	End of exposure practice	Duration of exposure practice
	Practice 1				

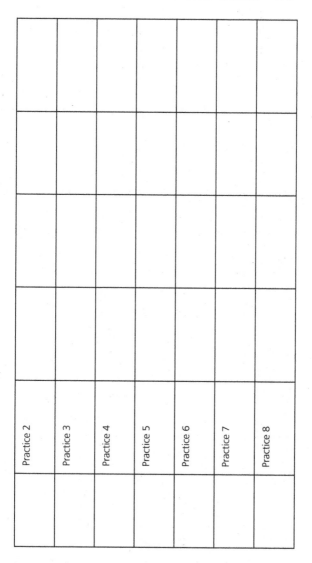

Practice 2					
Practice 3					
Practice 4					
Practice 5					
Practice 6					
Practice 7					
Practice 8					

Facing your Agoraphobia Record Sheet

Exposure Step	Details of your feared situation for this practice:			
Date and time of planned exposure practice	Exposure Anxiety Ratings (0-100)			
	Start of exposure practice	Highest level	End of exposure practice	Duration of exposure practice
Practice 1				

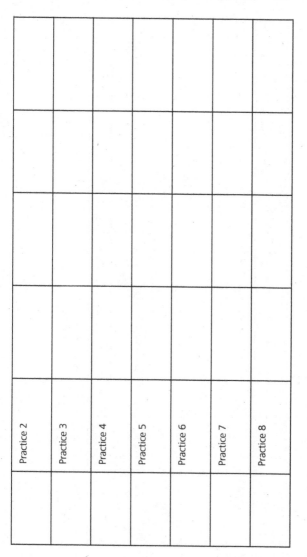

	Practice 2	Practice 3	Practice 4	Practice 5	Practice 6	Practice 7	Practice 8

Facing your Agoraphobia Record Sheet				
Exposure Step	Details of your feared situation for this practice:			
		Exposure Anxiety Ratings (0–100)		
		Start of exposure practice	Highest level	End of exposure practice	Duration of exposure practice
Date and time of planned exposure practice				
Practice 1				

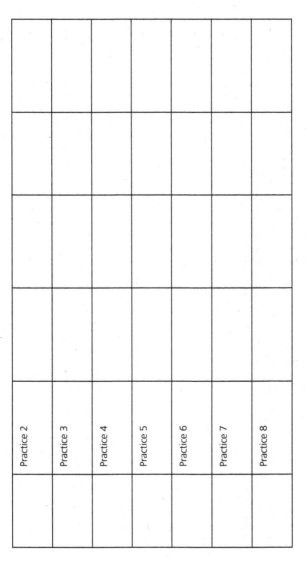

Practice 2	Practice 3	Practice 4	Practice 5	Practice 6	Practice 7	Practice 8

Facing your Agoraphobia Record Sheet

Exposure Step	Details of your feared situation for this practice:		
Date and time of planned exposure practice	Exposure Anxiety Ratings (0-100)		Duration of exposure practice
	Start of exposure practice	Highest level	End of exposure practice	
Practice 1				

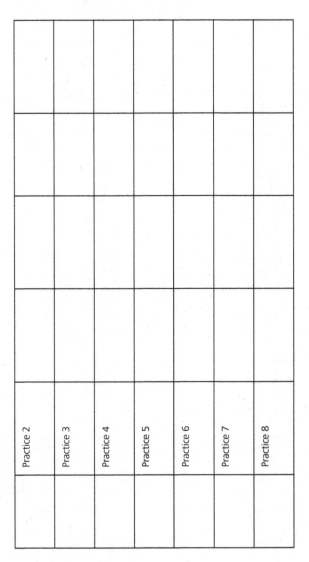

Practice 2	Practice 3	Practice 4	Practice 5	Practice 6	Practice 7	Practice 8

Facing your Agoraphobia Record Sheet

Exposure Step	Details of your feared situation for this practice:			
		Exposure Anxiety Ratings (0–100)		
		Start of exposure practice	Highest level	End of exposure practice
Date and time of planned exposure practice				Duration of exposure practice
	Practice 1			

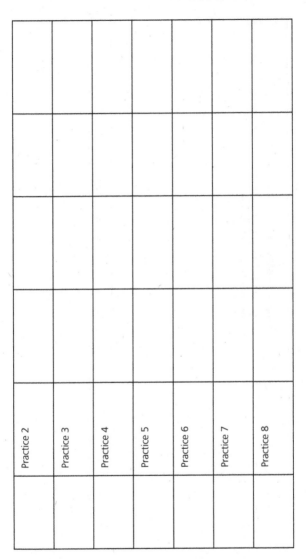

Practice 2	Practice 3	Practice 4	Practice 5	Practice 6	Practice 7	Practice 8

Facing your Agoraphobia Record Sheet

Exposure Step	Details of your feared situation for this practice:			
		Exposure Anxiety Ratings (0-100)		
		Start of exposure practice	Highest level	End of exposure practice	Duration of exposure practice
Date and time of planned exposure practice				
Practice 1				

Practice 2					
Practice 3					
Practice 4					
Practice 5					
Practice 6					
Practice 7					
Practice 8					

Facing your Agoraphobia Record Sheet

Exposure Step	Details of your feared situation for this practice:			
		Exposure Anxiety Ratings (0-100)		
Date and time of planned exposure practice	Start of exposure practice	Highest level	End of exposure practice	Duration of exposure practice
Practice 1				

Practice 2	Practice 3	Practice 4	Practice 5	Practice 6	Practice 7	Practice 8

My wellbeing review

Review date:

What have my symptoms been like over the past month?

Reading through my red flags list, have I had any experiences that have concerned me?

Do I need to take any action now to keep on top of my fear?

If so, what will be helpful to use in my toolkit?

What do I need to do and when am I going to do it?

The date of my next review is:

My wellbeing review

Review date:

What have my symptoms been like over the past month?

Reading through my red flags list, have I had any experiences that have concerned me?

Do I need to take any action now to keep on top of my fear?

If so, what will be helpful to use in my toolkit?

What do I need to do and when am I going to do it?

The date of my next review is:

My wellbeing review

Review date:

What have my symptoms been like over the past month?

Reading through my red flags list, have I had any experiences that have concerned me?

Do I need to take any action now to keep on top of my fear?

If so, what will be helpful to use in my toolkit?

What do I need to do and when am I going to do it?

The date of my next review is:

My wellbeing review

Review date:

What have my symptoms been like over the past month?

Reading through my red flags list, have I had any experiences that have concerned me?

Do I need to take any action now to keep on top of my fear?

If so, what will be helpful to use in my toolkit?

What do I need to do and when am I going to do it?

The date of my next review is:

My wellbeing review

Review date:

What have my symptoms been like over the past month?

Reading through my red flags list, have I had any experiences that have concerned me?

Do I need to take any action now to keep on top of my fear?

If so, what will be helpful to use in my toolkit?

What do I need to do and when am I going to do it?

The date of my next review is:

My wellbeing review

Review date:

What have my symptoms been like over the past month?

Reading through my red flags list, have I had any experiences that have concerned me?

Do I need to take any action now to keep on top of my fear?

If so, what will be helpful to use in my toolkit?

What do I need to do and when am I going to do it?

The date of my next review is:

Further information

The National Health Service (in the UK)

The UK NHS website has a summary of useful information about agoraphobia and panic disorder. The relevant links are:

https://www.nhs.uk/conditions/agoraphobia/

https://www.nhs.uk/conditions/panicdisorder/

This page https://www.nhs.uk/conditions/agorapho bia/treatment/ includes a video that describes how to refer yourself in England for psychological therapies and tells you what to expect.

The website also has details of other anxiety conditions. Reading through these should help you confirm whether your difficulties are symptoms of agoraphobia (rather than a different anxiety condition, panic disorder for example). The link below will also help you to determine whether you might be experiencing another anxiety condition as well:

https://www.nhs.uk/common-health-questions/ lifestyle/do-i-have-an-anxiety-disorder/

You can find a psychological treatment service in England by visiting www.nhs.uk and searching for 'psychological therapy services'.

Remember that your doctor will be able to discuss these things with you as well as support you in your CBT self-help. In England, they will also be able to refer you to a psychological wellbeing practitioner who is specially trained to support you in this way. Remember to keep your doctor informed of all the treatments you are involved in and all the healthcare professionals you are in contact with.

If you have suicidal thoughts and are planning to act on those thoughts, please access support from a crisis team which can be accessed in the UK through your GP, your local accident and emergency department or the police. Further information about crisis teams can be found on the Rethink website: https://www.rethink.org/advice-and-information/living-with-mental-illness/treatment-and-support/crisis-teams/

Voluntary organisations

Samaritans. This charity offers 24-hour emotional support by providing a neutral, sympathetic listening ear to people who are in distress. Call them on 116 123, email jo@samaritans.org or visit their website:

https://www.samaritans.org/how-we-can-help/contact-samaritan/

Mind. This charity also has some useful information about agoraphobia. Ellie's story can be found at: https://www.mind.org.uk/information-support/your-stories/escaping-my-agoraphobia/ Beth shares her story about being a carer for her mum who has agoraphobia: https://www.mind.org.uk/information-support/your-stories/how-to-cope-with-being-a-carer/

Private sector

If you would like to find a private CBT therapist (who will charge a fee for each session) you can use this website: https://www.babcp.com/Public/Accessing-CBT.aspx

ACKNOWLEDGEMENTS

Very many thanks to Professor Karina Lovell from Manchester University for kindly granting permission for her self-help manual to be used to inform this book.

Thank you to Andrew McAleer from Little Brown and Mark Papworth, the series editor, for asking me to write this book.

INDEX

Page numbers in *italic* refer to diagrams.